Ben Roethlisberger dives over
the goal line for a touchdown
in the second quarter.

Published by Triumph Books, Chicago.

Pittsburgh Post-Gazette

John Robinson Block, Publisher and Editor-In-Chief
David M. Shribman, Executive Editor and Vice-President
Susan L. Smith, Managing Editor
Mary C. Leonard, Deputy Managing Editor
Jerry Micco, Assistant Managing Editor/Sports

BOOK CREDITS
Sports Editor: Donna Eyring

PHOTOGRAPHERS
Peter Diana
Matt Freed
Lake Fong
Robin Rombach
Andy Starnes
John Heller
Annie O'Neill

PHOTO EDITORS
Larry Roberts
Doug Oster
Curt Chandler

Content packaged by Mojo Media, Inc.
Editor: Joe Funk
Creative Director: Jason Hinman

This book is available in quantity at special discounts for your group or organization.
For further information, contact:

Triumph Books
542 South Dearborn Street
Suite 750
Chicago, IL 60605

Chicago, Illinois 60605
Phone: (312) 939-3330
Fax: (312) 663-3557

Printed in the United States of America

Contents

It's only a game.

Pittsburgh Post-Gazette ✦ By David M. Shribman ✦ Executive Editor

That's what we would have said, here at the confluence of the three rivers, here in the City of Champions, here where the phrase "black and gold" is pronounced as one word, had the Pittsburgh Steelers lost the Super Bowl. Only a game. Nice to be invited, great just to be here, pretty good run, wasn't it?

But now that it's over, now that the Steelers have won, now that the commemorative pages and the souvenir newspapers and those horrible hats and Terrible Towels have been put away, in closets and drawers and (who knows?) maybe even in safe-deposit boxes, we can recognize the truth: This was never really just a game.

Never really a game — not the sport of football in general, not Super Bowl XL in specific. It was a statement: Of pride, to be sure. Of resilience, certainly. Of grit and courage and determination and strength and even of grace and elan. It was a statement about comebacks (and Pittsburgh is the city of comebacks) and loyalty (and Pittsburgh stands above the crowd in the number of natives still living in the place of their birth) and above all about what it takes to succeed in the 21st century (leadership, ingenuity, skill, intelligence). That's why football is Pittsburgh's game, and why the game's capital, for the next year on the calendar and for decades in the nation's imagination, is right here, here at the Forks of the Ohio.

Consider the obstacles these Steelers faced, along with the storied string of away appearances: An injury to their quarterback. The meltdown against Jacksonville. The Jerome Bettis fumble against Indianapolis. Consider what they accomplished: A Monday-night triumph against San Diego when their star quarterback was felled. A renaissance on defense after a three-game losing streak. An upset spectacular in the noisy confines in Indianapolis. A rout of the highly touted Broncos. A thrilling victory against the arrivistes from Seattle.

In the rush to the championship the most remarkable thing about these Steelers was what they weren't. They weren't fancy. They weren't flamboyant. They weren't quarrelsome. They weren't in trouble with the law, or with their wives, or with their coaches, or with anybody. They weren't show horses. They were workhorses. Taste of the city, if you know what I mean.

There was one other thing they weren't, and it is telling. They weren't named something besides the Steelers. That means more than you might think. Take some of the more famous teams in sports folklore and they had a catch-phrase that anchored them in time and place. The Miracle Braves (Boston, 1914). Murderers' Row (New York, 1927). Broad Street Bullies (Philadelphia, 1970s). We are Family (Pittsburgh, 1979). Idiots (Boston, 2004). These guys were just the Steelers, because what they did was what we expect them to do. Sports highlights videos often commemo-

Game MVP Hines Ward scores a touchdown against the Seahawks in Super Bowl XL.

(above) Willie Parker scores on the second play of the third quarter on a 75-yard run.
(opposite) Jerome Bettis rumbled for 43 yards on 14 carries in his final game as a pro.

uniform, the number 36 of our hearts. A sure-handed dreamboat (or so the ladies say, every one of them) from Georgia, wide receiver for the ages. A shaggy-haired strong safety from Southern California, the Zelig of the defense. And more. More and more and more.

Then there is the leadership. The coach: a scowling wreck of a man on the sidelines but perhaps the most gifted engineer in a city that respects, and trains, engineers. The owners: the canny older man, kindly but oh-so-shrewd, and his polished son, full of steely intelligence. Together they crafted a team, an ethic, a championship, a cult.

Now a word about the rest of us, we warriors of the couch. We attached our hopes, and our identities, to people we have never met but feel we know. Grown men and women shaped their daily routines — What time should we do the food shopping? — to be sure to be home to watch overgrown men play our homegrown sport. For this is Southwestern Pennsylvania's game because, like so many of the people who live here, it was born here, in Latrobe, in 1895. Southwestern Pennsylvania, mother of professional football. Never let it be forgot.

A half-century ago another Pittsburgh hero had some thoughts about the pioneering work he did — inside work, to be sure, but important work nonetheless. "Hope lies in dreams, in imagination, and in the courage of those who dare to make dreams into reality," said Jonas Salk, whose polio vaccine helped save so many so many years ago. Dreams, imagination, courage, and the daring to make dreams into reality — that is what we celebrate, this year and in the years to come, when we think of what this remarkable group of men — Steelers, Super Bowl Champions, 2006 — did in Detroit and for Pittsburgh. It's only a game, but still we dream. ■

rate a season of a lifetime. No one talked that way this year. This was simply the return of the natural order of things.

Not that there wasn't something extraordinary about this team, about this season, about this accomplishment.

Its achievement occurred not in the year it was supposed to happen, but in the year after that (unless, of course, you subscribe to the historically legitimate theory that, on the football field and in Pittsburgh, every year is the year).

This achievement was wrought by a remarkable group of men. A laser-disciplined quarterback from Ohio, embraced from the moment he stepped into town as Ours. A bruising running back with a soft heart, returned to Detroit for his greatest triumph but forever etched in our memories in a Steelers

High Five
A Riveting Run To Glory
Steelers 21, Seahawks 10 ✦ February 5, 2006 ✦ By Ed Bouchette

The Steelers' long search to repeat as Super Bowl champions ended after 26 years when they trumped the Seattle Seahawks, 21-10, at Ford Field.

Playing before a rollicking crowd dominated by Pittsburgh's black and gold, they won their fifth Vince Lombardi Trophy, tying the Dallas Cowboys and San Francisco 49ers for the most in the game's 40 years.

They capped a storybook run by winning their eighth consecutive game, became the first team to win three road playoff games and then the Super Bowl, and finished the Jerome Bettis saga in grand style.

"Our effort today made history," coach Bill Cowher said. "That's what made it special to me: This team has been real resilient all year. It was one guy after another. It's a tremendous group of guys."

Bettis, who rushed for 43 yards, raised the Lombardi Trophy and virtually announced his retirement in his hometown.

"I think the Bus' last stop is here in Detroit," Bettis told the crowd on the field after the game. "Detroit, you were incredible. Pittsburgh, here we come."

The Steelers flew home lugging their shiny, new silver booty to join the four trophies the franchise won in six years in the 1970s.

"We're so proud to bring it back to Pittsburgh," Dan Rooney said.

Wide receiver Hines Ward, who began training camp with a contract holdout, won the game's Most Valuable Player award after catching five passes for 123 yards, including a 43-yard touchdown from fellow wide receiver Antwaan Randle El.

"This is the one for the thumb," Ward said, holding his young son and, as usual, smiling. "We are bringing the Super Bowl back to the city of Pittsburgh."

Quarterback Ben Roethlisberger, who threw two interceptions and had a miserable 22.6 passer rating, nevertheless made plays when his team needed them. He dived into the end zone on third down for a touchdown in the second quarter and picked up another key first down in the fourth. In all, he ran seven times for 25 yards but completed just 9 of 21 passes for 123 yards.

Seattle halfback Shaun Alexander, the league MVP, was held to 95 yards on 20 carries.

The Steelers' halfback, Willie Parker, finished with 93 on 10 carries, most of that on one burst – a 75-yard touchdown run on the second play of the second half that was the longest in Super Bowl history and brought a 14-3 lead.

Parker ran a counter off the right. Pulling guard Alan Faneca, tackle Max Starks and guard Kendall Simmons threw big blocks, and Parker swooped through the line and was gone. Safety Etric Pruitt, playing for injured starter Marquand Manuel, made a diving attempt at Seattle's 40 to no avail.

Parker lit into the end zone, and the place erupted in a Terrible Towel windstorm.

Bettis is upended by Michael Boulware of the Seahawks. "We just brought a championship home," Bettis would say after the game. "One for the thumb."

"I just knew it was going to be a great play," Parker said. "They called it at the right time, and Faneca just paved the way."

The Steelers held the Seahawks, then moved in for what looked to be a coup de gras with a first down at the Seattle 11. After two Bettis runs moved them to the 7, wide receiver Cedrick Wilson flashed open behind cornerback Kelly Herndon on the right. But Roethlisberger woefully underthrew the ball right into the arms of Herndon, who returned it a Super Bowl-record 76 yards to the 20.

"That was one where my mind was telling me to throw it over the top and my arm didn't throw it over the top," Roethlisberger said. "I read it right. I just didn't throw it good."

Three plays later, Seattle quarterback Matt Hasselbeck threw a 16-yard touchdown to tight end Jerramy Stevens, and the shocking turnaround left the Steelers holding a tenuous 14-10 lead instead of what might have been a 21-3 stranglehold.

It fell so quiet in Ford Field you could hear the Seahawks fans.

It became deathly so a bit later when Stevens caught an 18-yard pass to the Steelers' 1 that put Seattle on the brink of snatching a fourth-quarter lead. But the play was canceled by a holding penalty and, on the next snap, nose tackle Casey Hampton sacked Hasselbeck at the 34. On third down, Hasselbeck threw deep and poorly. Cornerback Ike Taylor, who dropped an early interception, picked this one off to preserve the Steelers' four-point lead.

It would spark another celebration four plays later.

On third-and-2 at Seattle's 43. Roethlisberger ran 5 yards on a draw from the shotgun. On the next play, he pitched to Parker and threw a block. Parker handed off to wide receiver Antwaan Randle El, who ran to the right, stopped and uncorked a perfect pass that Ward caught over cornerback Marcus Trufant at the 5 and ran into the end zone for a 43-yard play.

It was the first touchdown pass by a wide receiver in the game's history, and it gave the Steelers a 21-10 lead with 8:56 left in the game.

"They called a great play at the right time," Ward said. "The offensive line did its job blocking, and El threw a hell of a ball."

The Steelers were fortunate to hold a 7-3 halftime lead. The Seahawks moved the ball offensively and smothered the Steelers on defense but had little to show for it, mainly because of untimely penalties.

"You can't make mistakes like that and expect to win against a good team like this," Hasselback said.

The Seahawks took a 3-0 lead with 22 seconds left in the first quarter on Josh Brown's 47-yard field goal, and the Steelers were lucky it wasn't worse They finally got something going after Ward ran 18 yards on a first down to their 48. But, on the next play, Roethlisberger faked to Bettis and threw a deep ball that floated and was intercepted by safety Michael Boulware at the 17.

On the Steelers' next possession, Roethlisberger converted a third down by throwing 20 yards to Wilson. Ward dropped what would have been a 22-yard touchdown pass, and a 10-yard penalty and sack pushed the Steelers back to the 40, facing a third-and 28.

Roethlisberger dropped back, scrambled away from a three-man rush and tiptoed up to the line of scrimmage. He stopped and heaved the ball deep toward the opposite side, to the right, the kind of play John Elway made famous. Ward outmuscled Boulware to make the catch at the 3.

Bettis got 2 yards on two carries and, on third down, Roethlisberger rolled left behind Bettis and plunged toward the goal line. The ball barely crossed into the goal line for a touchdown that was held up by a review.

It was the first time a Steelers quarterback scored in a Super Bowl.

The Steelers led, 7-3, and took that to halftime when Brown missed a 54-yard field goal wide with two seconds to go. Brown also would miss a 50-yarder in the second half.

"We're bringing the Super Bowl trophy back to Pittsburgh," linebacker Joey Porter said. "That's all that matters." ∎

SCORING BY QUARTERS

	1st	2nd	3rd	4th	Total
Seahawks	3	0	7	0	10
Steelers	0	7	7	7	21

A CLOSER LOOK

SEATTLE		STEELERS
20	FIRST DOWNS	14
5	Rushing	6
15	Passing	8
0	Penalty	0
5-17	THIRD DOWN EFFICIENCY	8-15
1-2	FOURTH DOWN EFFICIENCY	0-0
396	TOTAL NET YARDS	339
77	Total Plays	56
5.1	Average Gain	6.1
137	NET YARDS RUSHING	181
25	Rushes	33
5.5	Avgerage per rush	5.5
259	NET YARDS PASSING	158
3-14	Sacked-Yards lost	1-8
273	Gross-Yards passing	166
26-49	Completed-Attempts	10-22
1	Had Intercepted	2
5.0	Yards Per Pass Play	6.9
3-2-1	KICKOFFS-END ZONE-TB	4-0-0
6-50.2	PUNTS-AVERAGE	6-48.7
0	Punts blocked	0
0-0	FGs-PATs BLOCKED	0-0
174	TOTAL RETURN YARDAGE	99
4-27	Punt Returns	2-32
4-71	Kickoff Returns	2-43
2-76	TOTAL Interceptions-Return Yards	1-24
7-70	PENALTIES-YARDS	3-20
0-0	FUMBLES-LOST	0-0
33:02	TIME OF POSSESSION	26:58

RUSHING STATISTICS

SEATTLE

Alexander	20-95
Hasselbeck	3-35
Strong	2-7

STEELERS

Parker	10-93
Bettis	14-43
Roethlisberger	7-25
Ward	1-18
Haynes	1-2

PASSING STATISTICS

SEATTLE

Hasselbeck	26-49-1-273

STEELERS

Roethlisberger	9-21-2-123
Randle El	1-1-0-43

RECEIVING STATISTICS

SEATTLE

Engram	6-70
Jurevicius	5-93
Jackson	5-50
Stevens	3-25
Strong	2-15
Hannam	2-12
Alexander	2-2
Morris	1-6

STEELERS

Ward	5-123
Randle El	3-22
Wilson	1-20
Parker	1-1

PUNT RETURNS — YARDS

SEATTLE

Warrick	4-27

STEELERS

Randle El	2-32

KICKOFF RETURNS — YARDS

SEATTLE

Scobey	3-55
Morris	1-16

STEELERS

Colclough	2-43
Taylor	1-0

TACKLES — ASSISTS — SACKS

SEATTLE

Hill	7-1-0
Tatupu	6-3-0
Pruitt	4-0-0
Trufant	3-0-0
Bernard	2-0-0
Boulware	2-3-0
Wistrom	2-0-1
Lewis	2-2-0
Tubbs	2-0-0
Koutouvides	2-0-0
Kacyvenski	1-0-0
Hasselbeck	1-0-0
Darby	1-0-0
Dyson	1-0-0
Manuel	1-0-0
Herndon	0-1-0

STEELERS

Taylor	6-1-0
Townsend	5-1-0
Haggans	5-0-0
Farrior	4-2-0
Foote	4-1-0
Polamalu	4-1-0
Hampton	4-0-0
Porter	3-0-0
A.Smith	3-1-0
Keisel	2-0-0
Carter	2-1-0
Harrison	2-1-0
von Oelhoffen	2-0-0
McFadden	2-0-0
Hope	1-2-0
Kriewaldt	1-1-0
Iwuoma	1-0-0
Colclough	1-0-0

INTERCEPTIONS — YARDS

SEATTLE

Boulware	1-0
Herndon	1-76

STEELERS

Taylor	1-24

MISSED FIELD GOALS

SEATTLE

Brown	54 (WR), 50 (WL)

STEELERS

None

"This is a special group of coaches, a special group of players," Cowher said after winning Super Bowl XL. "I'm only a small part of it. We have a special organization and it starts at the top."

Perfect Start
Parker, Roethlisberger ignite romp against Tennessee
Steelers 34, Titans 7 ✦ September 11 at Pittsburgh ✦ By Ed Bouchette

That first-team Steelers offense that could not produce a touchdown this summer, that even had their head coach worried, could not be stopped.

They left summer stock to perform a smash Broadway hit as the Steelers played almost flawlessly on offense to throttle the Tennessee Titans, 34-7, and open the regular season in style at Heinz Field.

Ben Roethlisberger put every question about his poor preseason performance behind him in one quick swoop. He needed only 11 passes, the fewest thrown by the Steelers in nearly three decades, but completed nine for 218 yards, two touchdowns and no interceptions. He became the first NFL quarterback in two years to compile a perfect 158.3 passer rating.

Halfback Willie Parker also lived up to his "Fast" nickname and more, breaking tackles and spinning through holes on the way to 161 yards rushing, the 12th most by a Steelers runner, and that did not include the screen pass he turned into a 48-yard gain. The second-year back, making his first start, bowed out after three quarters, and it may take a lot more than healing by injured Duce Staley and Jerome Bettis to get him out of the starting lineup.

"He's got some big plays in him every time he touches the ball," marveled offensive tackle Marvel Smith. "If we give him a little bit of room, he can burst through the hole and make a lot of people miss him and take it to the house."

Parker did that on an 11-yard touchdown run in the third quarter, breaking two tackles along the way. Titans hit him on several occasions in the backfield, and he still eluded them. He had runs of 45 and 25 yards in addition to his 48-yard screen pass and averaged 7.3 yards on 22 carries.

"He's not more powerful, he's just faster and he's slick," said Titans defensive tackle Albert Haynesworth, whose grip on Parker slipped once in the backfield. "I mean, it was like the guy had Vaseline on or something."

Roethlisberger and his receivers looked pretty slick themselves, and, if they kept an offensive line rating it, too, would be perfect — Roethlisberger was not sacked and the Steelers piled up 206 yards rushing.

Everyone had reason to celebrate. Rookie tight end Heath Miller caught a 3-yard touchdown pass on his team's first drive. Jeff Reed tied Gary Anderson's team record by kicking field goals of 44 and 27 yards to give him 19 in a row without a miss. Antwaan Randle El, replacing the departed Plaxico Burress at split end, showed he can go deep, hauling in a 63-yard touchdown pass. Halfback Verron Haynes scored on a 5-yard run. And the Steelers defense had three sacks, two fumble recoveries and two interceptions.

"It was a great start," linebacker Larry Foote said.

Preseason? What preseason? Roethlisberger, who completed only 44.4 percent of his passes in the four

The Titans' Drew Bennett has a pass knocked loose by a hard-charging Ike Taylor.

(above) Kimo von Oelhoffen and Brett Keisel greet the fans as they head for the locker room after the Steelers' win over the Titans in their season opener. (opposite) Quarterback Ben Roethlisberger points to the sky after throwing a bomb to Antwaan Randle El for a 63-yard touchdown.

exhibition games and turned in a 32.8 passer rating, played better than he did when he broke Dan Marino's rookie records last season.

"He's going to get compared to last year and he's not going to live up to anybody's expectations with where he set the bar," Cowher said.

Actually, he exceeded that.

Cowher wasn't happy that his defense allowed the rebuilding Titans to drive 61 yards on the opening series to take a 7-0 lead on Steve McNair's 1-yard pass to tight end Ben Troupe. McNair (who finished 18 of 26 for 219 yards and a 91.7 passer rating) completed nine of his first 10, and the other one was dropped.

"We didn't start off very fast at all," Cowher said. "We didn't tackle real well in the beginning of the game."

Cowher said his team did not play "a very crisp game," but, after falling behind, 7-0, they burned Tennessee to a crisp.

How can Roethlisberger, Parker or anyone else on offense top this one over the next 15 games?

"I think for the most part it was a solid effort," Cowher said. "But we still have a long way to go." ∎

A closer look

Game 1	1st	2nd	3rd	4th	Total
Titans	7	0	0	0	7
Steelers	7	13	14	0	34

Tennessee		Steelers
16	First downs	18
3-8	Third down efficiency	5-10
303	Total net yards	424
97	Net yards rushing	206
219	Net yards passing	218
0	Sacks	3
4	Turnovers	0
7-49	Penalties/yards	3-27
29:10	Time of possession	30:50

Steelers Turn Up The Heat

Defense bags 8 sacks; Parker's running, Big Ben's passing lead to Texans' meltdown

Steelers 27, Texans 7 ✦ September 18, 2005 ✦ By Ed Bouchette

HOUSTON – On a sweltering Southeast Texas day, the Houston Texans chose to open their retractable roof, perhaps to avoid having the Steelers blow the top off Reliant Stadium.

The Steelers' march through the AFC South Division became Sherman-esque after they seared the Texans, 27-7, in a game where the temperature surpassed 100 degrees on the field in the sun. They have won their first two games, both against AFC South foes, by a combined 61-14 score.

"We're doing a lot of things we need to do to win football games," coach Bill Cowher said. It also was the first time in six years that the Steelers won their opening two games.

Quarterback Ben Roethlisberger wasn't perfect – he only looked that way as he completed 14 of 21 passes for 254 yards, two touchdowns to Hines Ward and a 139.8 passer rating. Willie Parker, getting the official affirmation from Cowher as the team's starting halfback, ran for a 10-yard touchdown among his 111 yards, his third consecutive 100-yard game. Jeff Reed set a Steelers record with two field goals to stretch his streak of success to 21.

And the defense clobbered Houston quarterback David Carr back into his rookie season. They sacked him eight times – three sacks were by Troy Polamalu to tie an NFL record for a safety – and had the quarterback talking to himself.

"He was running everywhere," said linebacker Joey Porter, who had his second sack of the season and came close on several more. "Delay of games, throwing the ball in the dirt, taking sacks, running into guys. He was scrambling for no reason at times. Sometimes, he sacked himself. He ran out of bounds on the line of scrimmage and he sacked himself."

As they did last week, the Steelers followed a formula developed last season: They took a lead, then ground the pulp out of the opposition. Roethlisberger threw 10 more passes than he did last week but only six came in the second half.

Roethlisberger shook off a sore left knee that made him questionable for the game and completed deep passes of 54 yards to Antwaan Randle El, 40 and 36 to Cedrick Wilson, and touchdown passes of 16 and 14 yards to Ward. The Steelers averaged 18.1 yards a catch.

Parker, making his second NFL start, set an early tone with a 19-yard run on the first play, starting the Steelers on their first drive that ended with Reed's 37-yard field goal.

Then it was time for the defense to set a tone of its own. On Houston's third play, linebacker Clark Haggans strung out a block by tight end Mark Bruener down the left side of the line, then swooped in to smack Carr's arm as he pulled back

Hines Ward breaks away from Texans free safety Marcus Coleman for a 16-yard touchdown pass at Reliant Stadium in Houston.

to throw. The ball popped loose, and Porter pounced on it at the Houston 22.

"I just reached out to try to hit his arm," said Haggans, who also had his second sack in two games. "The ball popped in the air, and Joey made a heck of a recovery."

Two plays later, Ward caught Roethlisberger's pass at the 8, broke one tackle and scored to put the Steelers ahead, 10-0.

One series later, Wilson caught a 36-yard pass and Ward caught four for 62 yards, including one in the middle of the end zone for a 14-yard touchdown and a 17-0 Steelers lead.

Randle El's 54-yard reception after Roethlisberger faked a handoff to Parker set up Reed's 35-yard field goal and a 20-0 halftime lead.

Carr threw a 3-yard touchdown pass to Domanick Davis to complete a 14-play, 78-yard drive by Houston to start the third quarter

The Steelers responded to Houston's only score by driving to their final touchdown. It came on Parker's run up the middle from 10 yards behind a Kendall Simmons block. The series got its jolt when Roethlisberger scrambled to his right, threw from the 30-yard line numbers all the way across to the left numbers, where Wilson caught it for a 40-yard pickup to the 23.

Cowher thought Roethlisberger could have picked up a first down by running on that play. So, too, did the quarterback. Call it inspiration, divine or otherwise.

"At the last minute, I think about running it, getting the first down, which I should have done," said Roethlisberger. "But then, I see Cedrick is going deep, and it occurred to me those guys are working hard, I was working hard with them all season, and we really just tried to put things together."

They have put them together the way Rembrandt might have. A thing to behold.

"It's week two, it's still early in the season,"

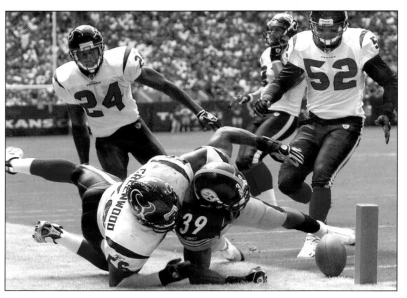

(above) Willie Parker is knocked out of bounds just short of the goal line by the Texans' defense. (opposite) Texans wide receiver Corey Bradford hauls in a pass over Ike Taylor in the second quarter.

Haggans warned. "There's a ton of football to be played, 14 games left, and we're still trying to create our identity. We're talking about building a foundation, building a house. Right now, we just probably laid the cement and put up the 2-by-4."

Right between the eyes of the Texans. ∎

A closer look

Game 2	1st	2nd	3rd	4th	Total
Steelers	10	10	7	0	27
Texans	0	0	7	0	7

Steelers		Texans
18	First downs	16
4-11	Third down efficiency	8-15
388	Total net yards	221
135	Net yards rushing	113
253	Net yards passing	108
8	Sacks	1
0	Turnovers	1
4-40	Penalties/yards	7-58
29:06	Time of possession	30:54

The One That Got Away

Randle El's errant lateral, key penalties set up Steelers' 23-20 last-second loss to Patriots

Patriots 23, Steelers 20 ✦ September 25, 2005 ✦ By Ed Bouchette

Tom Brady and Heinz Field go together like ketchup and fries, and New England's quarterback painted this town red again.

Hines Ward tied the score yesterday with his second touchdown catch with 1:21 left, way too much when it's on Brady time. The two-time Super Bowl MVP completed all 12 of his fourth-quarter passes, including three for 37 yards on the drive that set up Adam Vinatieri's 43-yard field goal with one second left and a 23-20 New England victory

"They're the Patriots," was Ward's explanation for what happened. "That's why they're champions. ... They just have Brady back there. He's the man. He's definitely the best in the league."

Brady didn't throw a touchdown pass and was sacked three times and threw one interception, but his performance was dominating. He completed 31 of 41 passes for 372 yards.

But it certainly wasn't unusual, and it has happened before at Heinz Field. Brady won for the third time in four games in Pittsburgh, four in five overall against the Steelers. If there was any consolation for the Steelers, at least this loss did not come in the AFC championship game as happened twice previously against Brady's Patriots.

"Better now than the AFC championship or the playoffs," said Steelers halfback Willie Parker.

Parker was bottled up for the first time in his young career. His streak of 100-yard games ended at three as the Patriots opened in a 4-3 defense and stayed with it most of the game.

Another streak, 16 winning games in the regular season, ended for the Steelers, who fell to 2-1 to match the Patriots' early record.

"It was a great run, but, for us, it's all about where we end up for the season," Ward said. "If this loss is going to make us better, so be it."

Quarterback Ben Roethlisberger, under tremendous pressure from a blitzing, confusing Patriots defense, completed 12 of 28 passes and was sacked four times. But those dozen covered 216 yards, and he threw touchdown passes of 85 yards and 4 yards to Ward

The 4-yard touchdown pass ended a 51-yard drive that tied the score when all seemed lost for the Steelers. But a 23-yard interference penalty on former Steelers cornerback Chad Scott, his second of the game, came on fourth-and-11 to put the ball at the 4.

"We gave ourselves a chance to win the ballgame," Ward said.

Ward was involved in many of the key plays as both teams scored on their first possession and then spent much of the first half squandering scoring chances with turnovers.

The Patriots converted their first drive when

The Patriots' Adam Vinatieri kicks a 43-yard winning field goal late in the fourth quarter to beat the Steelers at Heinz Field.

Corey Dillon scored from the 4.

It took the Steelers precisely 15 seconds to tie it. Roethlisberger quickly snapped off a pass to Ward, who got behind the Patriots' secondary and was never touched on his way to the longest pass play in Heinz Field history at 85 yards.

"Overall, we made plays when we had to," Ward said. "We didn't make enough, though."

The game also had a series of strange twists and turns that produced no points but plenty of drama.

With the Patriots at the Steelers' 14, Brady completed a screen pass to Kevin Faulk. But linebacker Clark Haggans fought off guard Stephen Neal's block, reached out and stripped the ball from Faulk. Larry Foote picked it up on a bounce and ran it 27 yards to the 35.

On second down, Roethlisberger struck. Antwaan Randle El caught a short pass and weaved neatly through New England's defense. Finally hemmed in near the 15, he spotted Ward following on the play and pitched him the ball. The surprised Ward, though, couldn't handle it, and New England recovered at the 11.

"We made eye contract," Randle El said. "If I could do it again, I think I would have kept it and tried to go in and score."

Later in the second quarter, Roethlisberger spun away from a tackle and threw the ball away, but linebacker Don Davis landed on him. Roethlisberger writhed on the ground, and it appeared his left arm was injured. He stayed down for several minutes, then slowly walked off the field.

Reed came on and kicked a 47-yard field goal. Tackle Barrett Brooks, however, was called for a false start, a 5-yard penalty. Cowher let Reed try again, but his 52-yarder was low and to the left, snapping his team record of 22 in a row.

The Patriots turned the ball back after reaching the Steelers' 5 when end Kimo von Oelhoffen tipped a Brady pass into the air and safety Chris Hope came down with it just before the half.

The Patriots, stung by turnovers in their loss to Carolina the previous week, continued their errant

(opposite) Hines Ward dashes for the longest passing play in Heinz Field history with this 85-yard reception from Ben Roethlisberger in the first quarter.

ways in the third quarter. Vinatieri sent a 53-yard field-goal try wide to the left.

Then the Haggans shell exploded again. He hit Faulk on a draw, causing his second fumble of the game. That turned into a 13-7 Steelers lead when Reed started a new streak, hitting a field goal from 24 yards.

Vinatieri didn't miss the next time. He hit from 48 yards. That closed the Steelers' lead to 13-10 late in the third quarter.

The Patriots jumped on top, 17-13, with 10:37 to go on Dillon's 7-yard touchdown run and stretched it to 20-13 on Vinatieri's 35-yarder with 3:19 left to set up the final dramatic back-and-forth finish.

"Their quarterback, Brady, has been there before," coach Bill Cowher said. "Unfortunately, he did what he's done many times before."

A lot of those times in Heinz Field. ∎

A closer look

Game 3	1st	2nd	3rd	4th	Total
Patriots	7	0	3	13	23
Steelers	10	0	3	7	20

Patriots		Steelers
24	First downs	14
8-16	Third down efficiency	3-13
425	Total net yards	269
79	Net yards rushing	79
346	Net yards passing	190
4	Sacks	3
3	Turnovers	1
10-118	Penalties/yards	5-35
35:23	Time of possession	24:37

Costly Injury?

Roethlisberger's knee injury puts damper on last-second 24-22 win

Steelers 24, Chargers 22 ✦ October 10, 2005 ✦ By Ron Cook

SAN DIEGO – By beating a very good San Diego Chargers team in a difficult environment in a city absolutely juiced by the "Monday Night Football" television cameras, the Steelers accomplished a couple of impressive feats.

They put themselves in position at the quarter-pole of the NFL season to win their division and maybe a whole lot more.

And they kept the collective citizenry of Pittsburgh from jumping into one of the three rivers.

The two go hand-in-hand, of course.

You think it was depressing around town after the Steelers lost at home to the New England Patriots?

It would have been downright unbearable if they hadn't found a way to survive the Chargers, 24-22, getting a 40-yard field goal from Jeff Reed with :06 left to do it.

The only downer on this otherwise magnificent night was quarterback Ben Roethlisberger's left knee injury on the winning drive. Defensive end Luis Castillo rolled up on Roethlisberger's leg, leaving him writhing in pain on the turf.

It was a shame to see Roethlisberger go down because this win was impressive in a number of ways. It kept the Steelers (3-1) even in the loss column with the Cincinnati Bengals (4-1) in the AFC North Division. It also kept them within sight of the Indianapolis Colts (5-0) in the race for home-field advantage in the AFC postseason tournament.

Hey, it's never too early to start thinking playoffs, right?

As much angst as that loss to the Patriots caused – you would have thought the world was ending if you listened to the talk shows – this win was so much more significant. It kept the Steelers from losing a second consecutive game, something they haven't done since midway through the 2003 season, an incredible span of 28 games. Another loss might not have destroyed the season, but it could have created just a bit of doubt on a team that fancies itself as a Super Bowl contender.

As it is, the Steelers are feeling mighty good about themselves this morning.

"I don't think this team will ever stop believing – regardless of the situation," defensive end Kimo von Oelhoffen said. "This is a tough football team."

The Steelers beat a strong opponent, a team good enough to roll over the Patriots and the New York Giants in its previous two games. And they did it in front of a boisterous crowd that had Qualcomm Stadium rocking.

The game was so big even Gov. Arnold Schwarzenegger showed up.

That's pretty big.

There were stars all over the lot for the Steelers.

There was Hines Ward, playing on a bad right hamstring, making catch after catch, six in all for 83 yards "I wasn't healthy at all, but there's no way I

Hines Ward blows by the Chargers defense during a Monday night game at Qualcomm Stadium in San Diego.

(above) Jerome Bettis wards off the Chargers' defense. (opposite) Linebacker James Harrison soars over the Chargers' LaDainian Tomlinson after intercepting a Drew Brees pass.

was missing a Monday night game," he said.

There was Roethlisberger, rebounding from a sub-par performance against the Patriots, beating the Chargers with his arm and his legs. He scored the first touchdown on a 7-yard quarterback draw.

There was Jerome Bettis, back in the lineup for the first time this season, making his presence felt in his usual, punishing way. He fairly danced for a 16-yard gain the first time he touched the ball on a screen pass and later scored on a 1-yard run. He also was huge on the winning drive, converting two third-and-1 plays. "That's the kind of guy he is," Bill Cowher said. "That's why you want him out there."

There was linebacker James Harrison, filling in for injured Clark Haggans, making one of the best interceptions and returns you'll ever see. He tipped a deflected pass to himself with his right hand, then rambled for 21 yards, looking like an Olympic hurdler along the way when he leaped over would-be tackler LaDainian Tomlinson.

There even was Heath Miller – yes, tight end Heath Miller – playing a big role in the offense that went far beyond just his blocking. He caught a 16-yard touchdown pass from Roethlisberger to give the Steelers a 21-16 lead in the fourth quarter.

It all made for marvelous theater.

Not to mention one terrific win. ∎

A closer look

Game 4	1st	2nd	3rd	4th	Total
Steelers	0	14	0	10	24
Chargers	0	7	6	9	22

Steelers		Chargers
25	First downs	20
4-10	Third down efficiency	5-12
311	Total net yards	279
104	Net yards rushing	66
207	Net yards passing	213
1	Sacks	3
1	Turnovers	2
11-104	Penalties/yards	9-100
33:23	Time of possession	26:37

The Heart And Soul Of The Steelers

By Gene Collier

Jerome Bettis barged out of the Heinz Field tunnel for the last time at 12:57 p.m. yesterday, high-stepping, fists clenched, a joyous ball of quick-twitch muscle fiber aching to command one final standing O.

Unless, of course, he didn't.

Unless, of course, it wasn't.

Unless he has another script in development, another way he'd like to leave this stage, some incredible cadenza that eclipses the three thunderclap touchdowns that broke down the door to the playoffs for a Steelers team that might not have done it without him.

"You take it for granted so many times, being in that tunnel," he said. "I was really concentrating, looking at the cracks, the way the lights look from there, looking at everything, just taking a kind of snapshot of it. Because when it's over, the only way you see the tunnel is from the outside looking in."

The more Bettis tried to explain his emotions and his plans in the hour after he dragged Bill Cowher's walking hangover of a football team past the Detroit Lions, the more it became clear that Bettis might not be sure which way he's facing in the dark psychological tunnel leading to life after football.

He reconfigured every question, lined them up randomly, shrugged them into postponement.

"At what point does your body fail you?" he said. "At one point are you less a player? At one point do you ask yourself, 'Am I in the way of this franchise going forward?' That's the last thing I want to do."

It was a lot more satisfying, presumably, to get in the way of a team going backward so fast it was backing right out of the playoffs. That's when Bettis grabbed a fourth-and-goal handoff at the Detroit 1 and slammed into the end zone behind fullback Dan Kreider for a 14-14 tie with the dreadful Lions as the first quarter expired.

At the end of a first half that saw Ben Roethlisberger deliver a stunningly flaccid 9.3 passer rating and Hines Ward fail to catch a pass, including the one that went through his hands and hit him in the face in the end zone, Bettis slashed 5 yards to the score that put the Steelers ahead, 21-14. His personal-best-tying third touchdown made it 28-14, and his 3-yard bash on third-and-1 sustained the drive that gave the Steelers another 14-point lead after the Lions had slashed it to seven, which pretty much left players and coaches on both sides in awe.

"I thought about falling down at the 1 so he could get a fourth one," said Roethlisberger, who scrambled 7 yards for Pittsburgh's final score. "I guess I didn't think fast enough."

Roethlisberger pointedly put off any discussion

The Bus rumbles for 25 yards in this fourth quarter run against the Bengals at Paul Brown Stadium in Cincinnati.

f Bettis' impact on this day, perhaps saving it for time more suitable.

"I can't talk about Jerome too much," he said. I'll get a little too emotional."

Cowher had come into the postgame news conference intent on praising his special teams nd looking toward the playoff-lurking Cincinnati Bengals, but when Bettis' name ropped, it put a severe strain on the head oach's emotions as well.

"I have so much appreciation for him; I think e's going to be one of those guys that when the lay comes that he's not here, there's going to be a oid there because it seems like he's always been here," Cowher said. "I have tremendous appreciation, more than I can ever express, for what he tands for as a football player but more so for what he stands for as a person. For every yard

that he's gained on the field, this guy, in my mind, has exceeded that off the field, the kind of individual he is, the way he gives back. I've neve been around too many guys like that."

Leave it to Bettis to bump the head coach hard toward eloquence, even toward tears.

When what was still very likely the last Pittsburgh crowd to see him perform finally got its playoff tickets punched, the swell of appreciation for No. 36 took on monumental dimensions It chanted "One more year!" It supplied a raucous, moving soundtrack to the Bettis runs lighting up the Jumbotron. It felt, and tried to fill wit its collective voice, the void Cowher anticipates.

"These fans have been my biggest supporters

s home his se

my whole career," he said. "The love was defi-
itely there, and I love them back."

It was, amid the raw brutality of this business,
n intensely poignant scene, so genuine it avoided
he game's lamest cliche. At one point, tackle
arrett Brooks went to the trainer's table and
icked up the big tub of Gatorade. He turned
oward Bettis.

"I saw him and said, 'No, don't even think
bout it,'" Bettis said. "I knew the big one might
e coming. As a running back, you have eyes in
he back of your head, so I was able to foil that

**Never one to shy away from emotion, Bettis exults in
the Steelers' victory over the Bengals.**

plot. That's why coaches always get nailed with i
They never hit a hole."

Of most head coaches, that is true, and so is
this. No one ever hit a hole harder than Bettis.
And that will be true for a long, long time. ∎

The Bus spikes the ball old-school style after plunging in for a score against the Colts in Indianapolis.

Gift-Wrapped

Overtime interception turns into winning touchdown as Jaguars steal 23-17 victory from Steelers

Jaguars 23, Steelers 17 ✦ October 16, 2005 ✦ By Ed Bouchette

It took them overtime to do so, but the Steelers finally convinced the reluctant Jacksonville Jaguars to accept their gift of victory.

No one tried harder than quarterback Tommy Maddox, who eventually succeeded. He fumbled away the Steelers' chance to win in overtime, then threw the touchdown pass that won it — when Jacksonville cornerback Rashean Mathis intercepted his offering and returned it 41 yards for the score with 11:24 left in overtime. That sent the Jaguars home from angry Heinz Field 23-17 winners.

Maddox, unhappy that he was booed at home several times, replaced injured starter Ben Roethlisberger, who pleaded before the game with coach Bill Cowher to play him.

"Coach's decision," said Roethlisberger, who watched the horror show from the sideline as the emergency No. 3 quarterback.

Cowher admitted he thought of changing quarterbacks at one point. Neither Charlie Batch, backup for a day, nor Roethlisberger, who could have entered the game in the fourth quarter, were told to get ready, although Cowher said it was "obvious" that Maddox had a bad game.

He completed 11 of 28 passes for 154 yards and a poor 30.1 passer rating. He threw one 16-yard touchdown pass to rookie tight end Heath Miller, but he lost four turnovers. Three were interceptions, and two led to touchdowns.

Before Mathis ended the game by stepping in front of a pass intended for Quincy Morgan, Maddox lost it.

Morgan's 74-yard kickoff return to open overtime gave the Steelers a first down at the Jacksonville 26, and it appeared to be over.

"I thought I gave us a chance to win," Morgan said.

With Jerome Bettis surprisingly kept on the sideline, Willie Parker lost 3 yards around left end, then gained 2 back. It was third down with the ball on the 27. From there, it would have been a 45-yard field goal to win it. But Cowher decided to get closer.

The call was a pitch to the right to Parker. Maddox took the snap from center Jeff Hartings and dropped the ball. He reached for it, seemed to kick it, and defensive end Reggie Hayward recovered at the 36.

"Everything felt good," Hartings said of his snap.

"I didn't get it clean," Maddox said, "and I don't know for what reason. I thought I had it, but I kind of bobbled it. When I was turning around, I thought I was about to control it and kind of bumped into [fullback Dan Kreider] and lost it. I was just trying to pick it up so I could just throw it away."

The victory raised the Jaguars' record to 4-2 and

James Harrison wraps up Jaguars quarterback Byron Leftwich in a physical game at Heinz Field.

left the Steelers in disbelief at 3-2.

"I'm certainly in shock," Hartings said. "We didn't handle the ball very well there at the end and didn't even give ourselves a chance to kick a field goal. That's definitely bad football."

"It hurts you," said receiver Antwaan Randle El. "These types of losses really hurt."

They thought they had it won a few times. Jeff Reed, whose only miss in his previous 26 field-goal tries came from 52 yards, missed just to the right on a 46-yard attempt in a swirling wind with 3:28 left in a tie game.

The Jaguars seemed poised for a victory with a first down at the Steelers' 34, but, on third down from the 32, rookie cornerback Bryant McFadden intercepted a Byron Leftwich pass in the end zone. It was the only turnover for the Steelers' defense.

"When you turn the football over four times and are minus-3 in the giveaway-takeaway ratio, you aren't going to win many football games," Cowher said.

Jacksonville used Maddox's first interception to erect a 7-0 lead in the first quarter.

Miller, who led the Steelers with four receptions for 72 yards, tied the score when he took a short pass over the middle and broke three tackles to bull his way to a 16-yard touchdown early in the second period.

Randle El returned a punt 72 yards to put the Steelers on top, 14-7. Following a deflected punt — the first in Chris Gardocki's career — Jacksonville's Josh Scobee kicked a 23-yard field goal after the Jaguars failed to score on three tries from the 1.

Jacksonville took a 17-14 lead on Leftwich's 10-yard pass to rookie wide receiver Matt Jones, and the Steelers tied it on Reed's 29-yard field goal in the fourth quarter.

That's when both teams played a game of "you

(above) Roethlisberger congratulates Antwaan Randle El after scoring a touchdown against the Jaguars. (opposite) Randle El tries to haul in a pass over the Jaguars' Rashean Mathias in the third quarter.

take it, no I don't want it" until the Jaguars stepped up and put an end to matters.

"We had our opportunities," defensive end Kimo von Oelhoffen said. "We didn't play smart football, both sides of the ball. Sometimes you get the bear, sometimes the bear gets you." ■

A closer look

Game 5	1st	2nd	3rd	4th	OT	Total
Jaguars	7	3	7	0	6	23
Steelers	0	14	0	3	0	17

Jaguars		Steelers
17	First downs	16
7-19	Third down efficiency	1-12
246	Total net yards	218
93	Net yards rushing	73
153	Net yards passing	145
2	Sacks	3
1	Turnovers	4
10-106	Penalties/yards	7-80
36:04	Time of possession	27:32

De-Clawed
Steelers' emphatic victory clear message to Bengals
Steelers 27, Bengals 13 ✦ October 23, 2005 ✦ By Bob Smizik

CINCINNATI – In the parlance of the day, the Steelers smacked the Cincinnati Bengals in the mouth. Then they smacked them in the mouth again. And again and again and again.

As for the Bengals, they smacked no one.

This game, built as an epic struggle for supremacy in the AFC North, turned into a colossal mismatch. The Bengals weren't up for the fight. In fact, they had no fight.

By virtue of five wins compiled against lightweight competition, the Bengals remain in first place in the division. But the Steelers' 27-13 manhandling of them at Paul Brown Stadium left no doubt as to which was the better team. Cincinnati might be in first place, but the Steelers (4-2) are the team to beat in the AFC North. The young upstarts weren't ready for the defending champs, weren't close to being ready.

The victory was vintage Steelers. A relentless rushing attack, led by Willie Parker's 131 yards, and just enough passing by Ben Roethlisberger provided all the offense that was necessary.

But this was a victory of defense. This was no second-rate outfit the Steelers held without a touchdown for the first 58 minutes. This was the No. 1 offense in the AFC, one that averaged 26 points per game. This was the team that had Carson Palmer, the man, some would have you believe, who is the next great NFL quarterback.

After the Steelers got through with him, Palmer remains the second best quarterback in the AFC North.

This game may well be remembered as the day Ike Taylor came of age as one of the elite cornerbacks in the NFL. In a move mindful of the way the Steelers used the great Rod Woodson, Taylor lined up wherever Pro Bowl wide receiver Chad Johnson was. Johnson caught four passes for 94 yards – 47 of those yards came on the meaningless late touchdown drive – and was not a factor in the game.

But the player the Steelers throttled the most was Palmer, who came into the game with a streak of 148 passes thrown over 18 quarters without an interception. That streak lasted 21 more passes and two quarters. Then on three throws early in the second half, Palmer had two passes intercepted.

The first was returned 58 yards by safety Chris Hope and set up a field goal. The second was snagged by defensive end Aaron Smith after Kimo von Oelhoffen tipped the ball and resulted in a touchdown that gave the Steelers a 17-6 lead.

End of game.

Not only were the Steelers ahead by 11, but the Cincinnati offense was finished. On the next three possessions, they gained 16 yards and had one first down.

"I just didn't play well enough to win," said Palmer, who completed 21 of 36 passes for 227

Troy Polamalu intercepted a fourth-quarter pass from Carson Palmer at the Bengals' 26-yard line and returned it for a touchdown.

(above) Willie Parker scampers into the end zone on a 37-yard run. (opposite) Chris Hope steps in front of the Bengals' T.J. Houshmandzadeh for an interception.

yards. "I gave them two turnovers, and in both of those situations they had great field position. When you play a championship team, you can't give them anything.

"It's my responsibility to put points on the board. I flat out didn't play well enough to win."

The Steelers' game plan for Palmer was simple: pressure, pressure, pressure.

"We knew in order to win this game we had to have a lot of pressure and force him to make bad throws," James Farrior said. "For the most part, we did that. He's a great quarterback. He's going to have better games. Today was our day."

Defensive coordinator Dick LeBeau, a former head coach of the Bengals, had some input.

"Coach LeBeau worked his magic and confused them," linebacker Larry Foote said.

Confusion helps, but the Steelers won this game with their play, not coaching strategy. They understood the challenge but also refused to allow it to become a dominant theme the week of the game.

"We're just not ready to give it up yet," Farrior said of the Steelers' AFC North dominance.

If they continue to play like this, they'll be dominating a lot more than the AFC North. ∎

A closer look

Game 6	1st	2nd	3rd	4th	Total
Steelers	0	7	17	3	27
Bengals	3	3	0	7	13

Steelers		Bengals
20	First downs	20
4-11	Third down efficiency	3-11
304	Total net yards	302
221	Net yards rushing	91
83	Net yards passing	211
2	Sacks	1
2	Turnovers	2
5-65	Penalties/yards	4-35
35:29	Time of possession	24:31

Thriller

Steelers learn that nothing comes easy in the NFL

Steelers 20, Ravens 19 ✦ October, 31, 2005 ✦ By Ron Cook

This one had a horrible feel to it from the start and quickly got worse. It was so bad into the fourth quarter that it was fair to wonder if Myron's Terrible Towels were going to be enough to save the Steelers.

They were, barely.

Maybe the Baltimore Ravens came into Heinz Field ticked that no one gave them a prayer of winning. Or maybe the Steelers — a whopping 11-point favorite — thought the Ravens had no chance. The reason really doesn't matter. The Steelers' 20-19 victory on Myron Cope Night was much more difficult than anyone could have imagined.

Not that your favorite team was complaining.

"I'll take a one-point win against those guys any day, all day, including holidays," Jerome Bettis said.

Well, it was Halloween.

The bottom line is the Steelers got a win that bumped their record to 5-2. That didn't just keep them breathing heavy on the Cincinnati Bengals (6-2) in the AFC North Division. It set them up for a big stretch run with a schedule that, at this point, looks ridiculously easy.

Not that the Steelers want to hear about easy games this morning.

"Nothing is easy about the National Football League," coach Bill Cowher said, fairly growling.

The Steelers certainly were thrilled to say goodbye to the Ravens. In the NFL, games that are supposed to be pushovers almost always turn out to be hair-pulls. On paper, the Ravens were badly over-matched. They didn't just come in with a 2-4 record. They were without six starters, including quarterback Kyle Boller, linebacker Ray Lewis and safety Ed Reed.

So what were the Ravens doing with a 19-17 lead with 2 minutes to go?

Blame the Steelers. Hines Ward had talked about their need to bring their "A" game to play the wounded, prideful Ravens, their most hated rival. As it turned out, they showed up with their "D+" game.

Quarterback Ben Roethlisberger was magnificent on the Steelers' opening drive, ending it with a 4-yard touchdown pass to Heath Miller. After that, he was mostly mediocre, at least until the final, winning drive.

The Steelers never really got their running game going against that shell of a Baltimore defense. "Eight men in the box," center Jeff Hartings said, shrugging.

Then, there were the many mistakes, almost too many to count.

A holding penalty by cornerback Deshea Townsend on a third-down incompletion kept alive a Ravens' drive that ended in a touchdown.

The Steelers wasted a 59-yard kickoff return by Quincy Morgan when a sack of Roethlisberger took them out of field-goal range.

The Steelers wasted an Ike Taylor fumble recov-

Willie Parker left the Ravens' defense gasping during a Halloween game at Heinz Field.

(above) Roethlisberger tries to escape from the Ravens' Kelly Gregg in the first quarter. (opposite) Ike Taylor (24) leaps high into the air to break up a pass intended for the Ravens' Randy Hymes.

ery at the Ravens' 12 when Roethlisberger took another sack, forcing them to settle for a Jeff Reed field goal.

Roethlisberger set up a Ravens' field goal by throwing an interception to defensive end Adalus Thomas.

Ricardo Colclough fumbled on a kickoff return at the Steelers' 29. The Steelers got lucky soon after when Matt Stover's 43-yard field goal attempt hit the right upright.

Then, there was what should have been the worst mistake. Punt snapper Greg Warren clanged the ball off upback Sean Morey's leg, giving the Ravens possession at the Steelers' 45 with 5:48 left. That set up Stover's 47-yard field goal for that 19-17 lead.

"At that point, I was thinking, 'If we're as good as we think we are, we'll pull this thing out,' " Hartings said. "Good teams find a way to survive."

And so the Steelers did.

Roethlisberger completed a 14-yard pass to Antwaan Randle El and a 23-yard throw to Morgan. After that, it was time for Reed, who kicked the winning 37-yard field goal with 1:36 left.

That sound you heard was the big Heinz Field crowd finally exhaling. Or maybe it was Cowher. ∎

A closer look

Game 7	1st	2nd	3rd	4th	Total
Steelers	7	3	7	3	20
Ravens	7	3	0	9	19

Steelers		Ravens
19	First downs	20
4-12	Third down efficiency	9-18
261	Total net yards	318
101	Net yards rushing	72
160	Net yards passing	246
2	Sacks	2
2	Turnovers	3
4-19	Penalties/yards	6-38
28:56	Time of possession	31:04

Favre's Favors

Packers quarterback's two turnovers help
Steelers walk away with 11th road win in a row

Steelers 20, Packers 10 ✦ November 6, 2005 ✦ By Ed Bouchette

GREEN BAY, Wis. – Statues of Vince Lombardi and Curly Lambeau tower over the main entrance to storied Lambeau Field. Inside they were joined by a third statue when the Packers' Brett Favre played as if he, too, were cast in bronze.

The Steelers, uninspiring on offense without quarterback Ben Roethlisberger and inconsistent on defense, stole away from Green Bay with a 20-10 victory that looked good only where it wound up, as their sixth win in eight games.

"It wasn't pretty," Steelers coach Bill Cowher acknowledged. "But we made enough plays to win the football game, and that's the bottom line."

Quarterback Charlie Batch, making his first start in four years, played that way, completing 9 of 16 passes for 65 yards, one interception and a 39.8 passer rating. Duce Staley (76 yards, 15 carries) and the running game helped bail out Batch with 154 yards rushing. But mistakes and the inaccuracy of Favre coupled with a few big plays on defense are what delivered the Steelers their club-record 11th consecutive road victory.

"Was it an ugly win? Yes," said receiver Hines Ward, who caught just one pass to leave him three from breaking John Stallworth's career team record. "Bottom line in this business is wins and losses; we're 6-2 at the halfway point."

They are there because safety Troy Polamalu turned

Favre's fumble into a game-changing 77-yard touchdown return, because Tyrone Carter's interception of a Favre pass led to the Steelers' only offensive touchdown, and because Favre did not have it in him to add to his 34 career comebacks.

"You have to know that he has a lot of comebacks in this game," linebacker Joey Porter said. "We kept coming after him, we kept pressure in his face. It worked out good for us."

Favre completed 20 of 35 passes for 214 yards and was sacked just once, and his running game was of little help with just 65 yards as the Packers slumped to 1-7.

The Steelers, outgained 268-213, converted none of their eight third-down plays.

"We didn't throw the ball for a whole lot of yardage," said Cowher, who insisted his game plan did not change much because it was Batch and not the injured Roethlisberger behind center. "We did not have a conservative approach. That wasn't the thinking coming in."

The Steelers managed little on offense in the first half but took a 13-3 lead on Polamalu's 77-yard fumble return and two field goals by Jeff Reed.

Batch threw short on a pass intended for Ward over the middle on the next series and linebacker Robert Thomas intercepted to give Green Bay a first down at the 36. Favre hit Donald Driver with a

Duce Staley straight-arms Packers safety Mark Roman en route to a 17-yard gain.

(above) Randle El picks up yardage against the Packers in the first quarter. (opposite) James Farrior wrestles down the Packers' Samkon Gado in the second quarter.

Cowher said. "It was huge."

The Packers finally scored a touchdown on another long drive to open the second half. Gado ran over from the 1 to cap a 65-yard drive and cut the Steelers lead to 13-10.

The 70,607 in Lambeau came alive, sensing another magical Favre moment.

Instead, Carter intercepted a pass, the Steelers took over at the 20, and four plays later Staley ran for a 3-yard touchdown.

Staley played so much because Willie Parker left the game with an ankle injury and Jerome Bettis already was out with a thigh bruise

"You can't even imagine the heart of this team," Staley said. "We all live on one heartbeat and that's how we're going to play the rest of the year." ∎

33-yard pass and the Packers had a first down at the Steelers' 3, looking to take the lead.

An incompletion, a 1-yard loss and consecutive false start penalties pushed them back to the 12. Defensive coordinator Dick LeBeau sent the blitz with Polamalu and rookie cornerback Bryant McFadden.

"It felt like I was going to a buffet," McFadden said. "My eyes got real wide, especially when I came free. I'm coming with as much attitude and aggression as possible. Not only to make a sack but to try to make him fumble like he did."

Favre spun away from Polamalu, but McFadden smacked into him, causing a fumble. Polamalu scooped it up, picked up a block from McFadden and ran 77 yards for a touchdown and a 13-3 Steelers lead.

"That stand, that's the series of the game,"

A closer look

Game 8	1st	2nd	3rd	4th	Total
Steelers	6	7	0	7	20
Packers	3	0	7	0	10

Steelers		Packers
13	**First downs**	16
0-8	**Third down efficiency**	8-17
213	**Total net yards**	268
154	**Net yards rushing**	65
59	**Net yards passing**	203
1	**Sacks**	1
1	**Turnovers**	3
4-53	**Penalties/yards**	8-74
26:52	**Time of possession**	33:08

Bill Cowher: Face Value

By Gerry Dulac

Deep down, when the blood begins to roil and the passion that can make a face wrinkle and a jaw tighten starts to churn, the player in Bill Cowher starts to emerge. Oh, he might look good for a while, standing there, arms folded, playing the part of head coach and remaining calm. But underneath the veneer that is as distinguishable as any visage in the National Football League, he is ready to blow, like Mount St. Helens, just one play from eruption.

It is then that Bill Cowher, 48, a kid from Crafton, can't contain himself. He will discard his headset in the same manner a hockey player drops his gloves, and he is off and running down the sideline, ready to mix it up with anyone he can find. He starts dropping in on sideline huddles, yelling at officials, alternately cheerleading his players as they come to the sideline or reprimanding those who have run afoul of his standards.

"You know what," defensive end Kimo von Oelhoffen said. "He's not a head coach. He's one of us. We consider him one of us."

In a world where idealism is often blurred with reality, Bill Cowher is undeniably a player's coach. He speaks their language, understands their job, knows when to back off, and, most important, has discovered the right way to push their performance button.

A former linebacker and special-teams standout who lasted only five seasons in the NFL, he understands the mental demands placed on players and the physical toll the sport extracts. Above all else, he believes in communication, never denying a player his right to express his opinion, even if it is a contrary one.

"I think he walks that line," said defensive end Aaron Smith. "He's got the respect of the players, but yet the players enjoy having him as a coach. He does a good job of keeping a fair balance between that."

"It's just the way he relates to the players," inside linebacker James Farrior said. "He's been on the other side, sitting where we are sitting. When he talks to us, we believe him."

Make no mistake, though. There is only one man in charge of the Steelers, and his name is William Laird Cowher.

"He's the reason this football team has been able to be so consistent through the years," running back Jerome Bettis said. "His philosophy and his makeup decide the makeup of this football team, so we're a physical bunch of guys, tough-minded, because he's a real reflection of that. He's been that way since the day I got here, and our teams have been reflective of that since the day I got here. I think he's been the driving force."

owher waves t

An exasperated Cowher pleads with the refs after a questionable call.

After 14 seasons with one of the most success-ul head coaches of the modern era, many of the teelers have heard Cowher's speeches so many mes that cornerback Deshea Townsend said, "I an probably finish the sentences for him."

Now they have heard the one speech they have ever heard before: The one following a Super owl victory.

Cowher had only one chance before – in 1995, when the Steelers lost to the Dallas Cowboys in uper Bowl XXX, the first time in five appear-nces the franchise had lost a Super Bowl game. ut it's not the loss for which Cowher was emembered. He was remembered for the num-er of times he didn't get to the Super Bowl.

Now, the coach of the Super Bowl Champion Steelers has cemented his legacy.

"It's a shame, but I think now people are start-ing to realize how good a coach he's been for how long," Bettis said.

Since the Super Bowl began in 1967, Bud Gran was only coach with more tenure with one team – 17 seasons with the Minnesota Vikings – not to win a Super Bowl. That's why Cowher was not satisfied merely making the Super Bowl for the second time in the past 10 years.

"Getting there is one thing, but it's not so much personal as it is for this organization, for these players and some of the guys that have been through some of the tough AFC losses in some o the AFC championship games," Cowher said.

In a season that has seen the Steelers win three playoff games by an average of 11.3 points and

Cowher has always had a strong bond with the players whom he coaches.

become the first No. 6 seed to reach the Super Bowl, Cowher is beginning to shake some of his playoff jinxes:

* He won his first road playoff game in four attempts when the Steelers beat the Cincinnati Bengals, 31-17, in the wild-card round.

* He won back-to-back playoff games for only the second time in eight attempts when the Steelers beat the top-seeded Indianapolis Colts, 21-18, in a division playoff games.

* And, after going 1-4 in AFC title games, he atoned for previous disappointments at Heinz Field with a convincing championship-game victory in Denver. The Steelers became the first team in NFL playoff history to defeat the Nos. 1, 2 and 3 seeds.

"You don't have the longest tenure in the league for a no reason," said wide receiver Hines Ward. "As players, you want to go out just to shut those people up who say he can't win the big one"

Super Bowl week in Detroit was XL for Bettis, a native of the Motor City who made it to the championship in what is expected to be his final NFL season. But it also was extra large for Cowher, who needed this Super Bowl win to crystallize his career, to bring into focus what he has done rather than what he has not. ■

Cowher and Hines Ward share a laugh in the first quarter of a Monday night game against the Eagles.

Second Batch
Veteran quarterback plays with efficiency of Big Ben, sparks big second-quarter romp
Steelers 34, Browns 21 ✦ November 13, 2005 ✦ By Ed Bouchette

Quarterback Charlie Batch not only replaced Ben Roethlisberger, but he also played like him, leading the Steelers to a 34-21 victory against the Cleveland Browns.

Batch left the game at halftime with a broken pinky bone in his right hand, but he did enough in those first two quarters to win his second start in a row in place of the injured Roethlisberger.

"He made good decisions, he looked confident and he made good throws," coach Bill Cowher said.

Batch completed 13 of 19 passes for 150 yards, and his quick move at the end of the first half might have saved a touchdown for the Steelers. His quarterback sneak with six seconds left gave them a 17-7 lead.

The Steelers climbed into a first-place tie with Cincinnati in the AFC North at 7-2.

"It's a good feeling," said linebacker Joey Porter, who had his fifth sack. "We haven't been there for a while."

After playing six close games, the Steelers ran away with one for the first time since Sept. 18 in Houston. They overcame a 7-0 deficit to take a 17-7 halftime lead. Reuben Droughns scored on a 5-yard run for Cleveland. Jerome Bettis and Batch each scored from a yard out, and Jeff Reed kicked a 42-yard field goal, all in the second quarter.

The Steelers broke it open on the third play of the second half. With Maddox at quarterback, Antwaan Randle El took a handoff from Duce Staley and threw a 51-yard touchdown pass to Hines Ward. It was Randle El's first pass attempt this season and second touchdown toss of his career.

Reed added a 33-yard field goal early in the fourth quarter, but his 44-yard attempt late in the game was blocked by Orpheus Roye and returned 59 yards for a touchdown by Leigh Bodden, who played at Duquesne University. Verron Haynes scored on a 10-yard run with 1:53 left, and Antonio Bryant caught a 9-yard touchdown pass from Trent Dilfer for Cleveland with 21 seconds left.

Ward caught eight passes for 124 yards. He passed John Stallworth with 543 career receptions for the team's record.

"He's caught a lot of passes here, and I've been here for every one of them," Cowher said.

Said Ward, "It was a great night for everybody ... a magical night."

Droughns' 5-yard touchdown run for the Browns was the fifth time in the past nine games a Steelers opponent scored a touchdown on its opening drive. The big play came when the Steelers blitzed six and Dilfer threw deep to Bryant. Cornerback Ricardo Colclough tripped and fell, allowing Bryant to catch it for a 35-yard gain to the Steelers' 17.

Four plays later, Droughns carried safety Chris

Deshea Townsend tries to break up a pass intended for the Browns' Braylon Edwards.

Hope on his back into the end zone for a 7-0 Cleveland lead.

The Steelers followed on their series with an apparent 20-yard touchdown pass from Batch to Ward. But Ward did not field the ball cleanly, bobbling it and then falling out of bounds. Browns coach Romeo Crennel challenged the touchdown ruling, and it was overturned by replay.

It cost the Steelers dearly because, on fourth-and-1 at the 11, they quickly lined up to go for it, and after a quick snap, Batch lurched forward but was stopped for no gain as the Browns took over. Cleveland could have jumped to a 14-0 lead but Dilfer badly overthrew to an open Braylon Edwards down the middle on third down to end its second series.

The Steelers finally tied the score on their first drive of the second quarter. Receiver Cedrick Wilson, who complained last week of not getting the ball enough, caught a 43-yard pass to the Browns' 12 when he came back on a ball that was thrown too short. Bettis, in the game for that series, ran 10 yards to the 2, and two carries later crashed into the end zone from the 1 for the touchdown.

The Steelers took a 10-7 lead on Reed's 42-yard field goal with 2:11 left in the second quarter. It was during that drive that Ward broke Stallworth's record with a 15-yard reception, and that is also the play in which Batch said his hand was broken when he hit a helmet. He stayed in the game and threw nine more passes and scored a touchdown before bowing out at halftime.

After Reed's field goal, the Steelers took advantage of Cleveland's hurry-up offense.

From his 22, Dilfer threw a pass that was tipped by safety Troy Polamalu, turning it into a pop-up that Porter intercepted.

Starting from the Browns' 40, the Steelers converted their first third-down situation in two games when Batch beat the blitz to complete a 14-yard pass to Ward. Ward converted another when he stretched out to catch a pass at the 7. Ward then caught a pass to the 1 and started celebrating in the end zone, thinking it was a score.

Hines Ward lays out for a ball and makes the catch against the Browns' Leigh Bodden.

With the clock running down and no timeouts left, Ward's teammates got his attention and, on third down, Batch sneaked in for a touchdown that made it 17-7 with six seconds left in the half.

The Steelers then scored on their next drive — the first of the second half — in spectacular fashion.

It came on the third play and on first down at their 49. Maddox handed off to Staley, who handed off to Randle El deep in the backfield. El made it look like a run, then threw deep to Ward. He caught the ball at the 10 as cornerback Ray Mickens trailed badly, and Ward completed the 51-yard touchdown.

"We got the corner to bite juuuuust enough," said Randle El, a quarterback in college at Indiana. "Yeah, I still got it. I still got my arm."

Late in the third quarter, Hope slammed into Bryant after a 21-yard reception, forcing a fumble. Bryant McFadden picked it up and ran 9 yards to the Cleveland 18. The Steelers turned that into three more points when Reed kicked a 33-yard field goal with 14:48 left.

The Browns closed to 27-14 on Bodden's 59-yard return with the blocked kick, but Cedrick Wilson recovered Cleveland's onside kick and Haynes ended a 29-yard drive by running for a 10-yard touchdown on fourth down. ■

A closer look

Game 9	1st	2nd	3rd	4th	Total
Steelers	0	17	7	10	34
Browns	7	0	0	14	21

Steelers		Browns
25	First downs	16
6-13	Third down efficiency	5-11
382	Total net yards	303
159	Net yards rushing	61
223	Net yards passing	242
2	Sacks	0
0	Turnovers	2
4-30	Penalties/yards	9-75
36:23	Time of possession	23:37

Road Wreck

Steelers hit a pothole as Ravens' overtime field goal caps sloppy game

Ravens 16, Steelers 13 ✦ November 20, 2005 ✦ By Ed Bouchette

BALTIMORE – In a game in which the drop kick returned to the NFL, the Steelers and Baltimore Ravens set pro football back half a century.

When they finally cleared the tangled mess that included 21 penalties, 11 sacks, four turnovers, numerous coaching blunders and other debris, the Ravens carted off a mild upset, 16-13, in overtime.

Matt Stover kicked his third field goal of the game, from 44 yards with 4:09 left in the 15-minute extra period, to win it.

Not only did the Steelers lose their second overtime game this season, but they also lost a chance to break out of a tie for first place in the AFC North with Cincinnati. The Steelers dropped to 7-3 as their 11-game road winning streak crumbled.

"It was a funky game," linebacker Clark Haggans said. "It was weird. It was just kind of everyone waiting for some kind of turning point, and it never came."

Oh, but it did. It came when Hines Ward performed the NFL's first drop kick in decades.

The Steelers tied the score, 13-13, on Willie Parker's 11-yard touchdown on a screen pass from Tommy Maddox with 5:15 left. They stopped the Ravens, got the ball back with 1:50 to go and were moving at midfield when Maddox threw toward Ward along the right sideline.

Ward leaped high over Chris McAlister, got his hands on the ball and, as he was trying to bring it in, the momentum threw it toward his foot as he

was going down. He inadvertently kicked it with his left foot high into the air, and linebacker Terrell Suggs made a diving interception.

"He was holding, they didn't call it," Ward complained of McAlister. "I tried to bat the ball down with my left hand, I batted it right to my foot and then it went up, and Suggs made a great play on it. It's one of those fluke instances that never in my life happened, and it happened today."

With a minute left, the Ravens went nowhere, and the game went into overtime.

Twice the Steelers had drives in overtime, but Maddox was sacked to end both drives.

The Steelers seemed to have the Ravens stopped again, but on third-and-10, Kyle Boller hit Randy Hymes with a 12-yard pass along the sideline to the Steelers' 44. The Ravens made another first down, and Stover came on to win it.

"I thought nobody was going to score actually in overtime," Porter said.

That's how poorly both offenses played.

The Ravens constantly blitzed Maddox, who made his second start and earned his second loss in overtime, and they ganged up to stop the run. The Steelers' ground game went nowhere with a season-low 70 yards rushing, and Maddox kept picking himself up off the ground. He completed 19 of 36 for 230 yards and that fluke interception. He also lost a fumble when his arm was hit as he was trying to throw.

Linebacker Clint Kriewaldt stops Ravens quarterback Kyle Boller for a short and painful gain.

Coach Bill Cowher could have challenged it except the Steelers had no time outs left because they frittered them all away by sending plays too late from the sideline or sending in the wrong packages.

"We were not real efficient on the sideline," Cowher admitted.

Said Maddox: "They came after us a lot, trying to stuff the run and the pass at the same time. We knew they only had three DBs back there so they had to get to me or we'd have our shots down the field."

They mostly got to him.

Typical of each team's offense was the way they scored a few times. The big play on the Ravens' first drive was a 15-yard penalty against James Harrison for roughing the passer. Stover converted from 47 on that series to post the first points of the game early in the second quarter.

Jeff Reed tied it when he kicked a 44-yard field goal on the next series, and Baltimore made it three series three scores when Hymes caught his touchdown pass. It looked as if some semblance of an entertaining game might break out.

But no. Jamal Lewis fumbled at his 20; the Steelers went nowhere after that and settled for another Reed

(above) **Willie Parker grinds out yardage against the Ravens.** (opposite) **Linebacker Clark Haggans hushes Ravens fans after a key stop on third down late in the game.**

field goal of 37 yards. Stover kicked another, from 25 yards, for a 13-6 halftime score.

The second half deteriorated into what can delicately be called bad football.

"We just didn't play well," Porter said. ■

A closer look

Game 10	1st	2nd	3rd	4th	OT	Total
Steelers	0	6	0	7	0	13
Ravens	0	13	0	0	3	16

Steelers		Ravens
17	First downs	18
4-15	Third down efficiency	7-20
282	Total net yards	241
70	Net yards rushing	104
212	Net yards passing	137
5	Sacks	6
2	Turnovers	2
10-62	Penalties/yards	11-70
34:00	Time of possession	36:51

Perfect Mess

Steelers become the undefeated Colts' 11th victim

Colts 26, Steelers 7 ✦ November 28, 2005 ✦ By Ed Bouchette

INDIANAPOLIS – The Indianapolis Colts' march toward NFL history rolled across the backs of the Steelers, who hung close for nearly a half before they became victim No. 11.

The Colts broke open a close game in the second half to win, 26-7. They ran their record to 11-0 in their attempt to become the first unbeaten NFL team since the 1972 Dolphins.

"No question, they're a great team, a great ballclub," receiver Hines Ward said.

The Steelers' season that once held so much promise now hangs on the brink.

After tying the second-longest NFL road winning streak at 11, the Steelers (7-4) have dropped their past two on the road. It's also their first two-game losing streak since they lost five in a row in 2003.

Indianapolis is the first team other than New England to beat quarterback Ben Roethlisberger. Back after missing three games following knee surgery, Roethlisberger played reasonably well, but he threw two interceptions, matching his season total entering the game. Roethlisberger completed 17 of 23 for 133 yards and was sacked three times.

The Steelers, eight-point underdogs, had to play nearly a perfect game to upset the Colts and they were far from it. They also figured they had to run on the Colts and they were unable to do that. Willie Parker had 43 yards rushing and Roethlisberger 21 as the Steelers managed only 86 yards on 25 carries.

It was their fourth game under 90 this season.

"When teams play 'cover-2' you're supposed to be able to run against them and we couldn't," Ward said.

Indianapolis did run, though, as Edgerrin James ended the Steelers' streak of 22 regular-season games without allowing a 100-yard rusher. He had 123 yards on 29 carries. The Colts outgained the Steelers, 366-197.

The Steelers' only touchdown came after Troy Polamalu intercepted a Peyton Manning pass and ran it back to the 7. Roethlisberger followed with a 12-yard touchdown pass to Ward near the end of the first quarter, and that was it. Jeff Reed missed a 41-yard field goal among many other failed opportunities for the Steelers.

"We weren't able to get anything going," said halfback Jerome Bettis, who had 9 yards rushing on six carries. "Obviously, nothing worked."

Manning threw touchdown passes of 80 yards to Marvin Harrison and 12 to Bryan Fletcher. The Colts' quarterback was not superb, but he was good enough. He completed 15 of 25 passes for 245 yards and he was sacked twice and threw one interception.

Mike Vanderjagt kicked four field goals for the Colts.

"Their defensive front pretty much dominated tonight, you can't deny that," Cowher said. "We just could never get anything going offensively and I think that wore on us defensively." ■

Ike Taylor breaks up a pass intended for the Colts' Marvin Harrison at the RCA Dome in Indianapolis.

A closer look

Game 11	1st	2nd	3rd	4th	Total
Steelers	7	0	0	0	7
Colts	10	6	7	3	26

Steelers		Colts
10	**First downs**	17
4-13	**Third down efficiency**	5-13
197	**Total net yards**	366
86	**Net yards rushing**	127
111	**Net yards passing**	239
2	**Sacks**	3
1	**Turnovers**	2
10-62	**Penalties/yards**	12-106
29:13	**Time of possession**	30:47

(above) Duce Staley is finally hauled down by the Colts' Gary Brackett and Raheem Brock. (opposite) Heath Miller, the Steelers' No. 1 pick in the 2005 draft, paid handsome dividends with 3 receptions for 61 yards and a touchdown against the Colts.

Is The Season Over?

Steelers drop the ball, put playoff chances in jeopardy with 3rd consecutive loss

Bengals 38, Steelers 31 ✦ December 4, 2005 ✦ By Ed Bouchette

After all the Steelers' fumbles and interceptions, the Bengals forced their most significant turnover in 15 years. The Steelers passed the AFC North torch, and Cincinnati intercepted it.

The Bengals held off the Steelers, 38-31, in their showdown at Heinz Field and left them trailing smoke in the division, two back with four to go.

"It's time for a change," Cincinnati receiver Chad Johnson said. "It's like going from a black and white TV to a color TV. It was Pittsburgh; it's Cincinnati now, and it'll probably be that way for a while now."

The Steelers, division champions in two of the past three years, slipped to 7-5 after losing their third consecutive game. The Bengals clinched their first winning season in 15 years at 9-3.

"They're not the Bengals of old," Steelers guard Alan Faneca said.

They've long been known as the Bungles, but that more appropriately described the Steelers' play yesterday. Ben Roethlisberger threw three interceptions, and his teammates fumbled four times, dropped passes, played poorly on special teams and contributed just the right amount of penalties to put the cherry on top of a loss that might well cause them to miss the playoffs.

"There were some obstacles that we created for ourselves that we just could not overcome," coach Bill Cowher said.

The Steelers mangled the Bengals in total yards, 474-324, but they also lost four turnovers and allowed a 94-yard kickoff return in the third quarter that killed the buzz among the crowd of 63,044 after Hines Ward tied the score with a 20-yard touchdown reception.

Roethlisberger threw career highs in every category: 29 completions, 41 attempts, 386 yards and three touchdowns. But then, so were his three interceptions, matching the number he threw in the AFC championship last January.

"I made too many mistakes. I'll take the blame," said Roethlisberger, who said his injured right thumb "hurts a little bit."

There was much blame to spread around, such as two fumbles by Willie Parker that prompted Cowher to yank him from the game, even though Faneca recovered both. Or the lost fumble on an end-around by Ward, who also dropped a pass at the goal line.

Despite all their mistakes, the Steelers got the ball back at their 24 with 2:26 left and trailing by seven.

"We still had a chance to win that game," Ward said.

If it weren't for a holding penalty against

(above) Hines Ward celebrates his touchdown in the third quarter. (opposite) Ike Taylor tosses Bengals wide receiver Chad Johnson to the turf after a catch.

Tyrone Carter on the Bengals' punt, they would have started at the 46. But that theme continued on their final series. On second-and-4, tackle Max Starks was penalized for a false start. On the next play, tackle Trai Essex was called for holding. On the next play, rookie linebacker David Pollack sacked Roethlisberger, who also was sacked on fourth down.

Game, set, and perhaps the 2005 match for the Steelers.

"I don't think right now we're the most confident team," center Jeff Hartings said.

There's also not much confidence left that the Steelers can win the division or make it to the playoffs.

"When you hit adversity, you see what type of players you have on your team," Ward said. "Who's going to quit? Who's going to keep fighting? The encouraging thing is we fought to the end."

It looked just like that, too. The end, that is. ∎

A closer look

Game 12	1st	2nd	3rd	4th	Total
Steelers	14	3	7	7	31
Bengals	7	14	7	7	38

Steelers		Bengals
28	First downs	21
6-13	Third down efficiency	6-14
474	Total net yards	324
95	Net yards rushing	102
379	Net yards passing	222
2	Sacks	1
7	Turnovers	0
7-70	Penalties/yards	4-30
33:18	Time of possession	26:42

Big Ben's Growth Takes Team To New Heights

By Bob Smizik

Anyone who said they expected this as they walked away from Heinz Field Dec. 4 after the Steelers lost their third consecutive game, is, to be kind, a fibber.

The Steelers were down and just about out after losing to the Bengals and before that to lowly Baltimore and Indianapolis. Worse, in the final two defeats their defense, the heart of the team, allowed 64 points.

There was a glimmer of hope they would make the playoffs, nothing more.

So how did it happen that there is the kind of jubilation throughout the city and the region that can only come with the Steelers going to the Super Bowl? How did it happen that the Steelers came back from those three losses to win seven in a row and in the process — with road victories — send home the third-, first- and second-seeded teams in the AFC playoffs?

It's no mystery. It has nothing to do with a change of coaching philosophy by Bill Cowher, as some have suggested. It has nothing to do with the us-against-the-world mentality the team has adopted.

It has everything to do with Ben Roethlisberger, who was excellent once again in directing the Steelers to a good, old-fashioned butt-kicking of the Denver Broncos, 34-17, in the AFC title game at Invesco Field.

For most of the Cowher era, the Steelers have been a championship-caliber team lacking only one thing: A championship-caliber quarterback.

Now they have one.

For the third consecutive playoff game, Roethlisberger was the dominant figure on the field, the major reason for victory. The team that for so long relied on the run, has come to rely on the pass. They depend on Roethlisberger, a 23-year-old, who, as Cowher said, "is a young quarterback who doesn't play young."

Roethlisberger did everything the Steelers asked of him, completing 21 of 29 passes for 275 yards and two touchdowns. His passer rating was a extraordinary 124.9. He made big play after big play — first in taking the Steelers to a 24-3 halftime lead and then in thwarting a comeback attempt by the Broncos by regaining the momentum for his team.

What is most remarkable about this performance is that for the second consecutive game Roethlisberger secured a victory with little or no help from the team's running game. While taking their 21-point halftime lead, the Steelers passed for 180 yards and ran for 49. For the game, they passed for 275 and ran for 90. They averaged only 2.7 yards per carry.

The team that for so long lived by the run is no more.

Boethlisberger showed no signs of a sophomore jinx in his second season as the Steelers' quarterback.

Big Ben will go all out for his team, as he did here for the game's only touchdown against the Vikings in Minneapolis. The Steelers won 18-3 and maintained their hold on an AFC wildcard berth.

"A lot of people said that if we have to throw the ball we can't win the game," Roethlisberger said. "Myself, the line, we took offense of that. The last couple of weeks, we've proven that's not the case."

"The pressure was on Ben to make some passes, to make some plays and he did," guard Alan Faneca said.

Linebacker Clark Haggans said, "He's been unbelievable. He's been the stable point of our

team, throwing the ball down the field, making plays. He's come a long way. He's so comfortable back there. He's a leader. He's a champion."

Roethlisberger has gone from being a quarterback along for the ride to one capable of putting a team on his shoulders.

"It seems like the light has gone on with him," offensive coordinator Ken Whisenhunt said. "Sometimes it happens late, sometimes it happens early. When he came back from the knee injury in our first game against Indy, he was struggling a little bit. From that point on [starting with a 386-yard game in the loss to Cincinnati] it just seemed like, 'I'm ready to go. Give me all you can give me.' "

The playoff-bearded Roethlisberger hugs teammate Hines Ward near the end of the game against the Broncos,

Big Ben has emerged as a fan favorite not just in Pittsburgh, but across the entire USA.

And that's what the Steelers have done. For the second consecutive game, they came out throwing and allowed Roethlisberger and his receivers to take control of the game.

That Roethlisberger has ascended to the elite of the league in only his second season, especially since he did not play in a high-profile college program, is a surprise to some, but not to Cowher.

"He's much more mature than his age would indicate," Cowher said. "He's very much in control. He's a great competitor. He's got a great feel for the game and a lot of self-confidence. I don't think he knows what not having success is."

The pressure will grow in the days ahead. Don't expect Roethlisberger to flinch or for Cowher to change his new game plan. The longtime advocate of the running game isn't turning back.

"We'll keep riding his coattails," Cowher said, "and, hopefully, there will be more to come." ∎

Roethlisberger celebrates after Hines Ward scores a touchdown in the first quarter in a 21-9 win against the Chicago Bears.

Bearing Down
Steelers pound Chicago in the mud and snow
Steelers 21, Bears 9 ✦ December 11, 2005 ✦ By Ed Bouchette

It doesn't require Einstein to write the Steelers' formula for winning: Get a lead, play good defense, run. No theory of relativity here.

The Steelers swerved from that time-tested equation for one reason or another in their previous three games, but they followed to a 21-9 victory against Chicago at Heinz Field.

No one compared the Bears' defense to their 1985 version after the Steelers bludgeoned them for 190 yards rushing, including two touchdown runs and 101 yards by Jerome Bettis, 100 of them in the snowy second half.

"We wanted to run it," coach Bill Cowher said.

Mixing screen passes, misdirection plays and the running of Bettis and Willie Parker against the aggressive Bears, the Steelers hopped to a 14-3 half-time lead. The plodding Chicago offense never made a game of it after that.

The victory ended a three-game losing streak — during which the Steelers did not rush for 100 yards in any game — to raise their record to 8-5. They gained no ground on victorious Cincinnati (10-3) in the AFC North and, with three games left, likely must chase one of two wild-card playoff berths in the conference.

"We live to fight another day," Cowher said. "We're a desperate team, and, right now, it takes desperate measures. We have to play like that every week. We have no margin of error."

The Steelers played as well as they have all season. They had no turnovers (nor did Chicago) and allowed no sacks. The Bears' rookie quarterback, Kyle Orton, threw for 207 yards but was sacked three times.

Parker added 68 yards to Bettis' first 100-yard game of the season. Ben Roethlisberger threw 20 times, completing 13 for 173 yards and one touchdown, a screen pass to Hines Ward that carried 14 yards to get them going.

"We just got back to what we do well — that's running the football, and it starts with the line," halfback Verron Haynes said.

Snow showers picked up early in the second half, to the Steelers' benefit. It helped negate the pass rush by Chicago, but there really was no need for one after the Steelers scored midway through the third quarter. They hardly passed after that.

Antwaan Randle El caught a leaping, 15-yard pass on third-and-14 to the Chicago 19. Quincy Morgan caught another on third-and-9 for 10 yards to the 8. The Bus came in and ran twice, the second time running over safety Mike Green and All-Pro linebacker Brian Urlacher on his way to a 5-yard touchdown.

It came with 7:01 left in the third quarter for a 21-3 lead. Roethlisberger threw just two more passes among 21 running plays the rest of the game. Bettis carried 16 times in the second half for

Willie Parker hurdles over the Bears' Todd Johnson during the Steelers' victory against Chicago.

(above) It was a winter wonderland for the Steelers in their game against the Chicago Bears, whom they kept in a deep freeze from the opening kickoff. (opposite) Randle El returns a kickoff in the fourth quarter.

A closer look

Game 13	1st	2nd	3rd	4th	Total
Steelers	7	7	7	0	21
Bears	3	0	0	6	9

Steelers		Bears
20	First downs	15
7-14	Third down efficiency	3-13
363	Total net yards	268
190	Net yards rushing	83
173	Net yards passing	185
3	Sacks	0
0	Turnovers	0
7-55	Penalties/yards	1-5
37:19	Time of possession	22:41

100 yards, including the Steelers' final six offensive plays.

Ward later told Bettis he was a "mudder."

"Hey," replied Bettis, "my mudder's a mudder, so that makes me a mudder."

The picture of Bettis on the sideline, the No. 36 on his jersey nearly obliterated by the grime from Heinz Field, is something he did not think would happen again.

"Absolutely not," he said, his 100 yards boosting his total this season to just 286. "My role is to come in and spell Willie, but this game set up for me in terms of the conditions and the field."

So, too, did the formula. ■

Eyes On The Prize
Determination, defense, doom the Vikings
Steelers 18, Vikings 3 ✦ December 18, 2005 ✦ By Ed Bouchette

The Steelers played in a dome for the second time this season, and it all happened again: The false starts, the turnovers, the confusion on offense, the mistakes. Only this time, it happened in the din of the Metrodome to the home team, the Minnesota Vikings.

The Steelers this time played like the team pumped up by noise as they rolled over the Vikings, 18-3, to end Minnesota's six-game winning streak and keep their own wild-card playoff hopes alive at 9-5 with two to go.

"We put ourselves in a hole through the year, so right now we have to fight for everything we get," linebacker Joey Porter said.

In that sense, Porter, linebacker Larry Foote and the rest of the Steelers' defense took the gloves off and mauled Vikings quarterback Brad Johnson and his offense. Porter had a sack, an interception and shared a safety with Foote, who had five tackles for losses. Cornerback Deshea Townsend intercepted Johnson in the end zone, and Minnesota managed only 54 yards rushing and 185 overall, both season lows for an opponent.

The Steelers' offense benefited from all this and also from a 72-yard punt return by Antwaan Randle El and a 49-yard run by Willie Parker, whose 81 yards spearheaded a 142-yard ground game.

Quarterback Ben Roethlisberger scrambled for a 3-yard run for the game's only touchdown, Jeff Reed kicked three field goals and Porter and Foote tackled Michael Bennett in the end zone for a safety for the Steelers. Paul Edinger kicked a 20-yard field goal for Minnesota's only points; Kimo von Oelhoffen blocked his 32-yard field-goal attempt.

"Our defense and special teams played so well today, they gave us good field position," said Roethlisberger, who threw only 15 passes, completing 10 for 149 yards and no interceptions. "They're so much fun to watch. I was on the sideline, jumping up and down. I have to be careful not to get a penalty out there, I'm out on the field half the time yelling and screaming.

The Vikings (8-6) committed five false starts on offense and drew three penalties for prematurely crossing the scrimmage line on defense.

Porter explained the false starts as "a little bit of nervousness over the pass rush that's going to come.

"When you have an offensive line scared of guys [they're] going against, they're going to false start because they want to get off early," Porter said.

The Steelers' defense, leading, 3-0, set the tone early after a muffed punt by Randle El gave the Vikings a first down at the Steelers' 3 in the first quarter. Cornerback Ike Taylor broke up a pass on first down and on third down at the one, Foote tackled rookie running back Ciatrick Fason for a one-yard loss. Edinger kicked a 20-yard field goal to tie the game, 3-3, and the Vikings never scored again.

Roethlisberger makes his decision and takes off on a 3-yard touchdown run.

(above) Larry Foote stuffs the Vikings' Ciatrick Fason. (opposite) Willie Parker picks up 14 yards on this fourth-quarter carry.

"Holding them to a field goal was huge in the beginning of the game," coach Bill Cowher said.

They did not hold them to field goals three other times they came into scoring territory – they shut them out.

What little offense the Steelers managed was enough. All they needed was a little after Randle El's 72-yard punt return gave them the ball on Minnesota's 14 in the second quarter.

Roethlisberger wanted to throw to Verron Haynes on third down at the 3, but held off, rolled left and looked for Randle El.

"I came back to the left side and saw the Red Sea open up and I took off running," the quarterback said.

Randle El threw a block, and Roethlisberger dived for the front left corner of the end zone. He stretched the ball out in his right hand, wearing a glove to help protect his injured thumb.

"At that point in the game, it was anything for a touchdown," Roethlisberger said. "I had to get it in. We had to score, and I was going to do whatever I had to get it in."

"If you want to play in January, you have to play your best football in December," Porter said. "It was good for our defense to go out and play back-to-back good games. It was a good stepping stone."

And yesterday's stone was carved from the Vikings' necks. ■

A closer look

Game 14	1st	2nd	3rd	4th	Total
Steelers	3	7	6	2	18
Vikings	3	0	0	0	3

Steelers		Vikings
14	First downs	11
5-15	Third down efficiency	3-12
275	Total net yards	185
142	Net yards rushing	54
133	Net yards passing	131
2	Sacks	4
1	Turnovers	3
12-129	Penalties/yards	13-95
36:48	Time of possession	23:12

Perfect Gift
The Steelers celebrate the season with a shutout
Steelers 41, Browns 0 ✦ December 24, 2005 ✦ By Ed Bouchette

After polishing off the Cleveland Browns as if they were Christmas cookies, the Steelers bolted home on the turnpikes knowing everything was back in hand for them.

Only the Detroit Lions in Heinz Field in one week separate the Steelers from a playoff berth, and they fully expect to pop some champagne on New Year's Day.

"We'll take some time, enjoy Christmas, come back Wednesday and understand what we have in front of us," coach Bill Cowher said. "We control our destiny. That's the only thing that counts."

By the time they stopped counting yesterday, the Steelers rang up the Browns, 41-0. Their first shutout in five seasons, combined with San Diego's 20-7 loss to Kansas City, left a clear path for the Steelers to earn the AFC's sixth and last playoff berth as a wild-card team outright if they beat the Lions to go 11-5.

"It's big, man," nose tackle Casey Hampton said. "It's a one-game season. We control our own destiny, you can't ask for anything else. That's what you play for."

Yesterday, they played like kids on Christmas morning, scoring on their first four series and leaving little doubt by the second quarter how this one was going to end.

Willie Parker put the cornerstone in this victory when he ripped through a gaping hole in the left side of the line and scorched 80 yards for a touchdown in the third quarter that put the Steelers ahead, 27-0, and put Parker over 1,000 yards rushing after picking up 130 against the Browns.

The Steelers sacked rookie quarterback Charlie Frye eight times and forced him to fumble four times. They outgained the Browns, 457-178.

"Pittsburgh played a great game today," Cleveland linebacker Ben Taylor said. "We got embarrassed on our own field."

Jerome Bettis ran 2 yards for a touchdown, Hines Ward caught a 7-yard pass from Ben Roethlisberger for his 11th touchdown catch, and Jeff Reed kicked field goals of 26 and 31 yards to stake the Steelers to a comfortable, 20-0 halftime lead.

Verron Haynes ran 15 yards for a touchdown in the third quarter, and Charlie Batch tossed a 31-yard touchdown pass to ex-Brown Quincy Morgan in the fourth quarter.

Roethlisberger completed 13 of 20 passes for 226 yards and no interceptions. Ward caught seven passes for 105 yards.

"They had a running back that we couldn't catch and a quarterback that threw pretty well," Browns coach Romeo Crennel said.

The Steelers dominated the Browns, beating them for the 11th time in the past 12 games.

"My Christmas is good now," Morgan said. "I don't need anything else for Christmas." ∎

Cedrick Wilson wraps his body around a pass in front of the Browns' Leigh Bodden during first-quarter action.

The Steelers posted their first shutout in five years against the Browns.

(above) Ward catches a touchdown in the second quarter against the Browns defenders. (opposite) Randle El leaps over the Browns' Nick Speegle.

A closer look

Game 15	1st	2nd	3rd	4th	Total
Steelers	14	6	14	7	41
Browns	0	0	0	0	0

Steelers		Browns
20	First downs	12
7-12	Third down efficiency	2-16
457	Total net yards	178
209	Net yards rushing	55
248	Net yards passing	123
8	Sacks	2
1	Turnovers	1
3-30	Penalties/yards	4-25
31:39	Time of possession	28:21

Rematch

The Steelers rely on special teams play to beat the Lions and march into the postseason

Steelers 35, Lions 21 ✦ January 1, 2006 ✦ By Ed Bouchette

The Steelers rang in the New Year, rang up the Detroit Lions and set a date for their rubber match with the Cincinnati Bengals. The winner moves on in the playoffs.

The sixth and final AFC playoff seed went to the Steelers because of their 35-21 victory against the stubborn Lions (5-11) at Heinz Field, their fourth consecutive victory.

The Steelers open the playoffs at in Cincinnati, the first postseason game between the teams.

"We wanted this game," linebacker Larry Foote said. "When we lost to them here, the feeling wasn't good. We got our wish."

The Bengals beat the Steelers, 38-31, Dec. 4 in Heinz Field. Cincinnati lost to them at home Oct. 23, 27-13.

"Bring 'em on. I can't wait," said defensive end Brett Keisel, who recovered a fumble on a punt return that led to a Steelers touchdown against the Lions. "I like playing against Cincinnati. I think we have something to prove."

They didn't play that way early yesterday against the Lions, who slipped to 18-point underdogs just before kickoff. The Steelers scored the first time they touched the ball on Antwaan Randle El's 81-yard punt return, but fell behind the Lions, 14-7, and led by just one touchdown with 51/2 minutes left in the third quarter.

"We weren't worried, but we were definitely concerned," Foote said. "The whole game, win and we're in, lose and we go home, so we were definitely concerned."

Their special teams' play, the running of Willie Parker and the run-scoring of Jerome Bettis helped them prevail on a day in which their defense sagged and quarterback Ben Roethlisberger threw two interceptions. Parker ran 26 times for 135 yards, and Bettis scored on three short touchdown runs, tying his career high on what likely was his final game in Heinz Field.

Ricardo Colclough's 63-yard kickoff return shortened the field for Bettis' first touchdown, a 1-yard run that tied the score near the end of the first quarter. Keisel's recovery of an Eddie Drummond fumble caused by Chidi Iwuoma on a punt return in the second quarter led to Bettis' second score, a 5-yard run in the second quarter.

"We didn't play well enough offensively and defensively, but I can't say enough about our special teams," coach Bill Cowher said.

The Steelers' defense, ranked third in the NFL, couldn't stop the Lions and quarterback Joey Harrington early on, who looked more like Joey Namath. Harrington, one of the lowest-rated passers in the league, threw three touchdown passes while completing 17 of 33 for 212 yards, no inter-

Big Ben dodges the Lions' Shaun Rogers to score a touchdown in the third quarter.

(above) The Lions' Eddy Drummond fumbles as Sean Morey (81), along with Brett Keisel (99) jump on the loose ball. (opposite) Jerome Bettis pauses at his locker after running for 3 touchdowns against the Lions.

The Steelers buried the Lions in the second half, 243 yards to 86, and actually stopped Detroit a couple of times on third down. The Lions converted 10 of 17 third downs, revisiting an old bugaboo for the Steelers.

"Third downs!" Cowher moaned. "We had third-and-19 and they converted, third-and-13 and they converted ... the things that we had been doing well, we did not do today. We have to rectify that."

Three drops of possible interceptions and just one sack.

His 11-yard toss to tight end Marcus Pollard tied the score after Randle El's second touchdown return of the season. Harrington put the Lions in front, 14-7, with a 1-yard scoring pass to fullback Cory Schlesinger two plays after a 63-yard pass to halfback Shawn Bryson.

By the half, the Lions had outgained the Steelers, 222-88, although the Steelers led, 21-14.

"We were not worried but more ticked off," said defensive end Kimo von Oelhoffen. "We are better than what we did early in the game. But we responded, I thought pretty good."

The second-half reversal began on the Steelers' opening drive when Hines Ward caught his only pass of the day for 40 yards that set up Bettis' third touchdown, a 4-yard run for a 28-14 lead.

Harrington threw his third touchdown pass, 15 yards to Roy Williams, but the Steelers responded on the next drive when rookie Heath Miller caught a 43-yard pass and Roethlisberger ended the day's scoring on a 7-yard scramble.

ceptions did not help, either – by Troy Polamalu, Foote and Ike Taylor. Those defenders tried to outdo the Steelers' receivers who could not hang onto the ball – Ward dropped one in the end zone, and Cedrick Wilson and Quincy Morgan also dropped passes.

They could make such mistakes and survive because they played the Lions. It should be a different story against the revived Bengals.

"They're playing at a high level," Cowher said. "They're explosive. ... We certainly have to play better than the last time we played them, and better defensively than how we played today." ■

A closer look

Game 16	1st	2nd	3rd	4th	Total
Steelers	14	7	14	0	35
Lions	14	0	7	0	21

Steelers		Lions
20	First downs	16
4-10	Third down efficiency	10-17
331	Total net yards	308
199	Net yards rushing	105
132	Net yards passing	203
1	Sacks	1
2	Turnovers	2
2-15	Penalties/yards	3-2
32:31	Time of possession	27:29

The Legacy
By Ed Bouchette

One for the thumb? Not for these Steelers, because they had none. Period. Dan Rooney compared their quest for their first Super Bowl ring to that of the 1974 Steelers, who also had never won a championship.

"I look at this as the first one," Rooney said. "It's the first one for this group of players, who really deserve it. They've really worked hard, they're really good football players, they played well.

"Not taking anything away from the guys back in the 1970s, but this is a new group, a new time."

The Steelers had not won a Super Bowl in 26 years, losing in their only previous appearance since then 10 years ago. They won four in six years, starting with the 1974 season.

"I would say this probably compares to our first time, Super Bowl IX," Rooney said. "It's very similar, these young guys we have, just like the players then. It's really their turn, their time up. The kind of people they are, it's a close team, they've done things the hard way, although it probably worked out, home and away."

Rooney is one of only four full-time Steelers employees who can get one for the thumb. Those with four Super Bowl rings include Rooney, running backs coach Dick Hoak, scout Joe Greene and Bob McCartney, their video coordinator. Longtime scout Bill Nunn has four, but he retired to part-time status.

"We're the last people who were here during that time," Rooney said. "It's really great to see this new generation come on, this generation of players, generation of coaches, it's really an exciting time. They've done well and they've earned it.

"I look at this as a separate thing; this is not one for the thumb, it's one for these guys."

Only one player on their 53-man roster had been to a Super Bowl – cornerback Willie Williams, who was on the Steelers' 1995 team. Line coach Russ Grimm has three rings from his playing days with the Washington Redskins and assistant secondary coach Ray Horton has one from Super Bowl XXVII with the Dallas Cowboys.

"It would mean a lot to me, but the thing I enjoy about it is seeing a lot of these guys who've never been there before," said Hoak, who will wear one or sometimes two of his four rings Saturday night before a game. "Now they're getting their opportunity. I get more excited about that.

Before the team left for Detroit, Rooney told his players in a meeting that the Steelers are proud of their past, but this is their time.

"He told us to play this one for us, and the things we've been through have nothing to do with the past," safety Mike Logan said. "Go out and play for ourselves.

"He definitely has the experience and he knows

The trophy from Super Bowl XIV seemingly towers over the skyline and fans in the "City of Champions."

Dan Rooney in the press box during the last game at Three Rivers Stadium. The Steelers played the Washington Redskins.

hat it's all about. I think he wants to make this n enjoyable time for us because he knows it's ectic with all the demands that come with the uper Bowl."

Rooney succeeded his father, Art, as team president in 1975 after the Steelers won their first Super owl. Son Art II succeeded Dan in 2002 and arned his first Super Bowl ring as the team's president, as his father and grandfather did before him.

"He's like these young players, really," Dan ooney said.

Rooney believes the excitement generated by his eam's march to the Super Bowl matches that of ne 1970s and comes at a good time for the city.

"I think it means a lot to Pittsburgh in so many vays," Rooney said. "It means something to pick ne town up, its feeling for itself, the idea we can o it. I think it's very meaningful when ittsburgh's trying to do a lot of things as far as

getting economic and labor employment going.

"You pick up a paper all over the world and people are saying the Pittsburgh Steelers are in th Super Bowl. It's a great team, and I think it's a great thing. Home playoff games would have produced much more money for the city, but this is something above and beyond the money."

Rooney believes the Steelers will compete for future Super Bowl berths.

"Sure, I definitely think we can continue to be successful. First of all, we look at this as — and rightly so — winning the Super Bowl is the ultimate. But you look at our team, what we've done in the last number of years. We've won more games than probably anybody. We've been in more postseason games, championship games and all those things. We've done well. I think these guys like it here, they're good people, all get along — at every level in this building. It's worked. I think we can go on." ■

top) "Mean" Joe Greene brings his four Super Bowls rings to camp as the Steelers, after four Super Bowl wins, pre
are to go for "One For The Thumb!" (bottom) Art Rooney Sr. stands in his team's locker room before practice.

(top) Art Rooney (bottom) Dan Rooney, Chuck Noll, Art Rooney Sr. and Richard Caliguiri celebrate after winning

(top) A crowd estimated at 4,500 jammed Market Square in downtown Pittsburgh to celebrate the Steelers' victory over the Dallas Cowboys in Super Bowl XIII in 1979. (bottom) Art Rooney and his son Dan look over their draft options in the Pittsburgh war room. The Steelers selected Franco Harris that year, a bruising fullback from Penn State who would go on to become a Pittsburgh legend.

One For The Road
Steelers overcome rough start, eliminate Cincinnati in playoff opener
Steelers 31, Bengals 17 ✦ January 8, 2006 ✦ By Ed Bouchette

The Steelers first took out quarterback Carson Palmer and then took out Cincinnati, 31-17, to end what the Bengals hoped would be a deep playoff run.

The comeback victory from a 10-0 deficit pits the Steelers against the Colts in Indianapolis for a 1 p.m. AFC semifinal playoff.

Palmer, No. 2 in the NFL passer ratings, left the game for good after completing a 66-yard pass on Cincinnati's second offensive play. Defensive end Kimo von Oelhoffen hit him low as he was throwing, which tore the anterior cruciate ligament in the quarterback's left knee.

Veteran Jon Kitna replaced Palmer and guided the Bengals to leads of 10-0 and 17-7, but the Steelers eventually pressured him into four sacks and two interceptions as their offense came alive behind quarterback Ben Roethlisberger.

"Carson Palmer's a Pro Bowl quarterback," Steelers coach Bill Cowher said. "Certainly, it's very tough when you lose a guy of that nature. You can't diminish that."

Roethlisberger threw three touchdown passes: 19 yards to Willie Parker, 5 yards to Hines Ward and 43 yards to Cedrick Wilson. Jerome Bettis ran 5 yards for another touchdown, and Jeff Reed kicked a field goal as the Steelers scored 24 consecutive points starting late in the second quarter.

The teams split their two regular-season games in the AFC North this season with the Bengals winning the division title. After Cincinnati won in Heinz Field Dec. 4, some Bengals declared that the torch had passed to a new team in the division.

"The torch never left," Ward declared. "They won one game, we finished with the same record. They won the AFC North, but, when it counted in the playoffs, I guess we kind of got the torch back."

Ward said that, "Cincinnati's our home away from home" after the Steelers won here for the seventh time in the past eight games.

Roethlisberger completed 14 of 19 passes for 208 yards, three touchdowns, no interceptions and a gaudy 148.7 passer rating. He was sacked once while turning in a marvelous playoff performance after two poor ones at the end of his rookie season.

"He made some big plays," Cowher said, "some big scrambles, and very good decision-making."

Bettis led the Steelers with 52 yards on 10 carries. Rudi Johnson led the Bengals with 56 yards on 13, including a 20-yard touchdown run that staked them to a 10-0 lead in the first quarter. T.J. Houshmandzadeh's 7-yard touchdown catch from Kitna in the second quarter gave the Bengals a 17-7 lead, but it was all downhill for the home club from there.

"We had to come out and weather the storm," Roethlisberger said. "They gave us a great shot in

Hines Ward makes a second-quarter reception in front of the Bengals' Deltha O'Neal.

the beginning, really pounded it to us, made some big plays. We said, let's keep scoring points when we can and take their best shot. I think we did that. We weathered it well."

Palmer was injured after he completed the longest pass in Bengals postseason history, a 66-yarder down the right sideline to Chris Henry, who beat cornerback Deshea Townsend.

Behind Kitna, the Bengals moved from their 22 to the 5, where Tyrone Carter tackled Houshmandzadeh on third down to force a field goal, converted by Shayne Graham for a quick, 3-0 Cincinnati lead.

The Bengals made it two drives, two scores to go ahead, 10-0. Kitna completed consecutive passes of 11 and 14 yards, scrambled for a dozen and then found Kevin Walter for a 15-yard pass to the 20.

Rudi Johnson broke off the left side, through Chris Hope's attempt to tackle him at the 15 and into the end zone for a 20-yard touchdown.

The Steelers' offense finally put it in gear early in the second quarter. Parker scored on a 19-yard screen pass from Roethlisberger, and it was 10-7.

Cincinnati hardly was finished, though. Kitna

(above) Jerome Bettis churned out 25 yards in the 4th quarter. (opposite) Troy Polamalu drags down the Bengals' Rudi Johnson for no gain.

completed a pass to a wide-open Houshmandzadeh for a 7-yard touchdown and a 17-7 lead in the second quarter.

Roethlisberger and the Steelers, though, responded. The quarterback pumped once and then pumped again and hit Cedrick Wilson with a 54-yard pass down the left side to the 22. Antwaan Randle El followed with a 16-yard catch that put the ball on the 6. On third down, Roethlisberger gunned a ball over the middle to Ward for a 5-yard touchdown that kept the Steelers in the ballgame, trailing, 17-14, at halftime.

"We felt at halftime we had taken their best shot," Cowher said. "There were so many positive things coming from their side, and it was only 17-14. That's not bad."

Cincinnati tried to stretch its lead when Graham attempted a 33-yard field goal in the third quarter. Brad St. Louis, however, snapped the ball high, and the Steelers took over at the 34.

That mistake triggered a turnaround as the Steelers took their first lead 41/2 minutes later.

Roethlisberger threw deep to Randle El, who beat safety Kevin Kaesviharn but dropped the perfect pass in the end zone. Kaesviharn, however, was flagged for pass interference on the play, giving the Steelers a first down at the 5.

Bettis took it from there, bursting through a big hole between left tackle and left guard and boring into the end zone for a 21-17 Steelers lead with 5:07 to go in the third quarter.

"The big guy still has some pretty good feet," Cowher said.

The Steelers used some razzle-dazzle to push their lead to 28-17 on their next drive. The center snap went to Randle El, who lined up to the left of Roethlisberger in the shotgun formation. He ran to his right, stopped and threw back to Roethlisberger at the Steelers' 45. Roethlisberger then passed deep to Wilson, wide open at the 5, for a 43-yard touchdown.

"We definitely needed a knockout punch," Wilson said. "It was a great call." ∎

The Bus drives into the end zone for a third-quarter score. (opposite) Deshea Townsend defends as the Bengals' Chris Henry hauls in a first-quarter pass.

A closer look

AFC Wild Card	1st	2nd	3rd	4th	Total
Steelers	0	14	14	3	31
Bengals	10	7	0	0	17

Steelers		Bengals
19	First downs	19
6-11	Third down efficiency	9-16
346	Total net yards	327
144	Net yards rushing	84
202	Net yards passing	243
4	Sacks	1
0	Turnovers	2
6-39	Penalties/yards	7-90
28:57	Time of possession	31:03

Whew!

Steelers breathe a sigh of relief after a thrilling 21-18 victory against Colts

Steelers 21, Colts 18 ✦ January 15, 2006 ✦ By Ed Bouchette

Move over Immaculate Reception, you have some company.

The Steelers head to Denver for the AFC championship game after their most improbable ending to a playoff game since Franco Harris ran into history in 1972.

They survived the Indianapolis Colts, 21-18, because quarterback Ben Roethlisberger made a game-saving tackle and the Colts' Mike Vanderjagt, the most accurate field-goal kicker in NFL history, missed badly from 46 yards with 17 seconds left.

"I don't need too many more of those feelings," receiver Hines Ward said, "but it's good to come out on the right side. You thought the game was over, your season was over and then the guy missed the field goal."

The game appeared over when linebacker Joey Porter sacked quarterback Peyton Manning on fourth down at the Colts' 2 with 1:20 left and the Steelers ahead by three. It was the fifth sack of the NFL's leading passer in the game.

Because the Colts had three timeouts left to stop the clock, the Steelers sent Jerome Bettis off right guard to try to put it away.

"We score there, and the game's over," coach Bill Cowher said.

But linebacker Gary Brackett slammed into Bettis and put his helmet on the ball. The man who rarely fumbles fumbled for the first time this season.

The ball popped backward. Cornerback Nick Harper, playing with three stitches in his right knee where his wife allegedly stabbed him the day before, picked it up. He had one man to beat to run 93 yards for the go-ahead touchdown — Roethlisberger.

"It's one of those things that once in a blue moon Jerome fumbles, and once in a blue moon I'm going to make that tackle," Roethlisberger said.

The quarterback who had not made a tackle in two NFL seasons got in front of Harper then tackled him by the foot as tight end Jerame Tuman came in to finish him off. For all the punishment the Steelers dealt to Manning and the Colts' offense yesterday, a tackle by their quarterback was the most important of all.

"That might be the biggest play ever in his career," linebacker Larry Foote said. "My heart was going to my feet and back up."

Still, the Colts and Manning had the ball at their 42 with 1:01 left. They reached the Steelers' 28, where rookie cornerback Bryant McFadden broke up a pass in the end zone to Reggie Wayne on second down and knocked away another for Wayne on third.

Vanderjagt came on to do what he does better than anyone: Convert a field goal and send it to overtime.

"Not today," Foote said.

Vanderjagt's attempt went wide, and the Steelers became the first No. 6 playoff seed to knock off a No. 1 seed.

"That was one of the craziest games I have been

Roethlisberger made perhaps the pivotal play of the season for the Steelers when he awkwardly tackled the Colts' Nick Harper after a Bettis fumble late in the fourth-quarter.

in," Porter said. "It feels good for the ball to actually bounce our way one time."

The Steelers, winning for the sixth consecutive time, overcame 10-point odds to a team that beat them, 26-7, here Nov. 28. The Colts were favorites to win the Super Bowl.

"A day ago, nobody wanted to give us a chance," Ward said. "We came out and we did what we had to do. ….They beat us pretty good the last time. This is kind of redemption for us."

The Steelers stunned the Colts and the noisy RCA Dome crowd when they took a 14-0 lead in the first quarter on Roethlisberger's touchdown passes of 6 yards to Antwaan Randle El and 7 to rookie Heath Miller.

Roethlisberger was hot, hitting 6 of 7 on the first scoring drive and connecting with Ward for a 45-yard pass on third-down that set up the second touchdown. He would throw only five times in the second half, completing 14 of 24 on the day for 197 yards.

When many expected the Steelers to run and control the clock, they came out throwing. They ran 13 times in the first half, and Roethlisberger threw 19 times and completed 12 in the first two

Larry Foote stops the Colts' Edgerrin James at the 1-yard line late in the second quarter. (opposite) Troy Polamalu tries to recover his own fumble after he apparently intercepted a pass thrown by Colts quarterback Peyton Manning in the fourth quarter.

quarters as the Colts dropped one safety back and kept everyone else but their cornerbacks close to the line of scrimmage.

"I knew they were going to give us eight guys in the box," coordinator Ken Whisenhunt said, "and they were going to play to stop the run. And our quarterback is really maturing, and he's understanding what we're trying to do."

Roethlisberger threw his only interception, in the first half, when he was hit by Dwight Freeney. But the Colts did nothing with that, much the way they spent the first three quarters. Manning (22 of 38, 290) threw off target, his passes sailing on him. The Steelers seemed to rattle him with both their blitzes and their disguised non-blitzes. Indianapolis managed only Vanderjagt's 20-yard field goal in the first half.

"I think we pressured them a lot more," Foote said. "Coach [Dick] LeBeau whipped up some new magic,

(above) Troy Polamalu jumps into the arms of Brett Keisel after his fourth-quarter interception was ruled incomplete. The NFL later admitted they made a mistake on the call. (opposite) Bettis celebrates after his touchdown.

at the Steelers' 48 with 5:26 left.

But Colts coach Tony Dungy challenged it, and referee Pete Morelli overturned it, saying Polamalu dropped it, even though he did not drop it until he stood up after making the catch and before a Colts player touched him.

The Steelers were incensed..

"The world wanted Indy to win so bad, they were going to do whatever they had to do, man," Porter claimed. "… I didn't think the refs were going to let us get out of here with a victory."

The Colts, given new life, continued on the series that ended with Edgerrin James' running 3 yards for a touchdown. Manning's pass to Wayne for the two-point conversion drew the Colts to within three with 4:24 left, and the Dome rocked again.

When Porter sacked Manning twice in three plays, dropping him at the 2 on fourth down, it was all over. Except for a few plays at the end.

"I know a couple of times our players were ready to celebrate prematurely," Cowher said.

That they finally got to do so was a wonder in itself. ■

gave them something nobody's seen yet."

The Steelers seemed poised to put the game away after linebacker James Farrior's booming sack on a blitz of Manning put the ball on the Colts' 1 on fourth down. The Steelers took over on the Indianapolis 30 after the punt and ran six times in a row — Willie Parker on an 11-yard scoot to start it and then Bettis five times for the other 19, including the final one up the middle for a touchdown that bounced them in front, 21-3.

Cowher's record is 100-1-1 in the regular season when his team leads at any point by more than 10. That did not seem to be in jeopardy even when Manning threw a 50-yard touchdown pass to Dallas Clark early in the fourth quarter.

And safety Troy Polamalu appeared to settle matters when he made a diving interception of Manning

A closer look
AFC Divisional Game

	1st	2nd	3rd	4th	Total
Steelers	14	0	7	0	21
Colts	0	3	0	15	18

Steelers		Colts
21	First downs	15
6-14	Third down efficiency	3-13
295	Total net yards	305
112	Net yards rushing	58
183	Net yards passing	247
5	Sacks	2
2	Turnovers	0
2-8	Penalties/yards	9-67
34:52	Time of possession	25:08

Super Highway

The playoff Bus heads for Detroit and a date with Seattle

Steelers 34, Broncos 17 ✦ January 22, 2006 ✦ By Ed Bouchette

DENVER – The Steelers proved again yesterday, there's no place like away from home, unless you're Jerome Bettis and that's where you're headed – home, to Detroit, to Super Bowl XL.

After losing four AFC title games in Pittsburgh over the previous 11 seasons, the Steelers left home to seek their fortune. They found it when they mauled the favored Denver Broncos, 34-17, to win their second conference championship in the past 26 years.

They became the second team in history to win three consecutive playoffs on the road to land in the Super Bowl and can become the first to follow with a world championship.

"The toughest route they said to take was the scenic route, and that ended up being the best route for us," declared linebacker Joey Porter, who had a monster game. "We went to three different cities and shocked the world three different times. We weren't supposed to be in this situation, but we pulled it off. We pulled it off everywhere we went."

They have one more stop, in Detroit, against NFC champion Seattle. It's a trip that helped lure Bettis, the fifth-leading rusher of all time and the heart of the Steelers the past decade, to play one more season, give it one more try to get to his first Super Bowl, to make his last game the one in his hometown.

He talked to his teammates Saturday night and left them with this:

"Get me home," the Bus said.

They punched that ticket early, stunning the Broncos by scoring on all four of their possessions in the first half for a 24-3 lead. Denver cut it to 10 midway through the fourth quarter, but the Steelers maintained their control and began celebrating when quarterback Ben Roethlisberger rolled left into the end zone for a 4-yard touchdown that sealed it, 34-17.

"Once Ben scored, I think everyone cut loose a little bit because we were up by so much with so little left," guard Alan Faneca said. "Everybody knew it was over, and we were excited."

Bettis and Duce Staley dumped the traditional bucket of Gatorade on Bill Cowher's head, and the sopping wet coach gave a big hug to Dan Rooney on the sideline. It has been 10 years since they have made this trip, 26 since they won a Super Bowl.

"We need to go and win the game," Cowher said. "Nobody ever remembers the loser in the Super Bowl."

The Steelers became the first sixth seed in the playoffs to reach the Super Bowl, and they did it by knocking off Nos. 3-1-2 in that order. They did it again in Denver before thousands of Terrible Towel-waving Steelers fans who also showed up in

Cedrick Wilson celebrates after the Steelers defeated the Broncos 34-17 in the AFC championship game, earning a trip to Detroit for Super Bowl XL.

(above) Roethlisberger dives into the end zone for a 4-yard touchdown in the fourth quarter. (opposite) Hines Ward tries to escape the grip of the Broncos' Nick Ferguson and Champ Bailey in the third quarter.

droves in Cincinnati and Indianapolis the two previous weeks.

"I know the fans here are going crazy," receiver Antwaan Randle El said. "It must be really crazy at home ... It is amazing, especially to have done it all on the road."

Once again, their young quarterback was the catalyst. The Steelers found it tough to run on Denver and managed only 90 yards on the ground, the first time this season they have won a game with fewer than 100 yards rushing. Roethlisberger and his receivers more than made up for that. He completed 21 of 29 passes for 275 yards, two touchdowns, no interceptions and two sacks for a 124.9 passer rating, his third striking performance in the playoffs.

"He's the catalyst of our offense," said Hines Ward.

Jeff Reed kicked a 47-yard field goal to get things

going, and the Steelers never stopped. Cedrick Wilson scored on a 12-yard pass, one of five receptions for 92 yards.

Bettis put the finishing touches on an 80-yard drive by running 3 yards for a touchdown. Ward completed the first-half blitzkrieg by catching a 17-yard touchdown pass.

The Broncos' only score of the first half came on Jason Elam's 23-yard field goal. They did score two touchdowns in the second half on Ashley Lelie's 30-yard reception from Jake Plummer and Mike Anderson's 3-yard run.

But Reed kicked another field goal from 42 yards, and Roethlisberger stilled any overbeating Steelers hearts when he put it away with his 4-yard run.

"The offense won this game," defensive end Kimo von Oelhoffen said.

Denver coach Mike Shanahan, who embraced Cowher on the field after the game, was impressed.

"Anytime you go into somebody's back yard and you beat the first, second and third teams and you do it throughout the playoffs, you can be very impressed," he said.

(above) Casey Hampton dives to recover a fumble in front of the Broncos' Cooper Carlisle and Jake Plummer in the first quarter. (opposite) Big Ben hands off to Willie Parker in the first quarter.

Reed's 47-yard field goal that got things going came after Denver cornerback Champ Bailey dropped an interception near midfield with no one in front of him.

The defense set up the Steelers' first touchdown when, three plays after the field goal, Porter smacked into Plummer, who fumbled. Casey Hampton recovered at the Broncos' 39.

Roethlisberger completed a 24-yard pass to tight end Heath Miller to the 14. On third down, Wilson faked inside, and Bailey bit on it. Wilson cut outside, and Roethlisberger delivered a perfect pass in the back corner for a 12-yard touchdown and a 10-0 Steelers lead on the first play of the second quarter.

Elam's 23-yard field goal gave the Broncos some light, albeit brief.

The Steelers responded with a 14-play, 80-yard drive that took 7 minutes, 28 seconds, and ended with Bettis running for a 3-yard touchdown behind the block of Faneca. It was the same play that produced the infamous Bus fumble last week.

Bettis' touchdown made it 17-3 and growing. Taylor intercepted his first pass on the next play from scrimmage on a Plummer attempt along the sideline to Stephen Alexander.

The Steelers began at Denver's 38, and Parker ran twice for 24 yards. Bettis scored from 12, but Ward's penalty for an illegal formation brought it back to the 17. Ward redeemed himself on the next play when Roethlisberger scrambled away from pressure to his left, threw across his body over two defenders into the back of the end zone where Ward caught it for a 17-yard touchdown with seven seconds left in the half.

"He had a small window to get it there and he got it in that window," Ward said.

The Steelers led, 24-3, the Broncos faithful booed their team as it left the field and the talk in the locker room was "don't take the pedal off the gas," Faneca said.

Denver scored its first touchdown late in the third quarter on a 30-yard pass from Plummer to Lelie.

A 30-yard pass from Roethlisberger to Wilson helped set up Reed for a 42-yard field goal and a 27-10 Steelers lead early in the fourth quarter.

Denver's Charlie Adams returned the kickoff 47 yards to the Steelers' 43, but on the next play, Foote intercepted Plummer.

The Broncos, though, still had life as Plummer hit Lelie for 38 yards, Taylor was called for a 22-yard pass-interference penalty, and Anderson ran in from the 3 to cut the lead to 10 with 7:52 left.

Not to worry. Brett Keisel crashed into Plummer, who fumbled. Travis Kirschke recovered at Denver's 17, and Roethlisberger drilled the final stake into the Broncos.

"Getting there is good," Dan Rooney proclaimed of the Super Bowl, "but we're going there to win. This is just another stop." ∎

(above) Broncos' quarterback Jake Plummer had nowhere to run and nowhere to hide against the Steelers' defense. (opposite) Jerome Bettis and Rian Wallace shower Cowher with the obligatory Gatorade dump after their team defeated the Broncos 34-17 in the AFC championship game, earning a trip to Detroit for Super Bowl XL.

A closer look
AFC Championship

	1st	2nd	3rd	4th	Total
Steelers	3	21	0	10	34
Broncos	0	3	7	7	17

Steelers		Broncos
20	First downs	16
10-16	Third down efficiency	5-11
358	Total net yards	308
90	Net yards rushing	97
268	Net yards passing	211
3	Sacks	2
0	Turnovers	4
8-61	Penalties/yards	4-20
36:07	Time of possession	23:53

STEELERS ROSTER

No	Name	Pos	Hgt	Wt	Birthday	Exp	College
3	Jeff Reed	PK	5-11	232	4/9/79	4	North Carolina
7	Ben Roethlisberger	QB	6-5	241	3/2/82	2	Miami (Ohio)
8	Tommy Maddox	QB	6-4	219	9/2/71	9	UCLA
16	Charlie Batch	QB	6-2	216	12/5/74	8	Eastern Michigan
17	Chris Gardocki	P	6-1	192	2/7/70	14	Clemson
20	Bryant McFadden	CB	5-11	190	11/21/81	R	Florida State
21	Ricardo Colclough	CB	5-11	186	4/18/82	2	Tusculum
22	Duce Staley	HB	5-11	242	2/27/75	9	South Carolina
23	Tyrone Carter	FS	5-8	190	3/31/76	6	Minnesota
24	Ike Taylor	CB	6-1	191	5/5/80	3	La.-Lafayette
26	Deshea Townsend	CB	5-10	190	9/8/75	8	Alabama
27	Willie Williams	CB	5-9	194	12/26/70	13	Western Carolina
28	Chris Hope	FS	5-11	206	9/29/80	4	Florida State
29	Chidi Iwuoma	CB	5-8	184	2/19/78	5	California
31	Mike Logan	SS	6-1	211	9/15/74	9	West Virginia
34	Verron Haynes	HB	5-9	222	2/17/79	4	Georgia
35	Dan Kreider	FB	5-11	255	3/11/77	6	New Hampshire
36	Jerome Bettis	HB	5-11	255	2/16/72	13	Notre Dame
39	Willie Parker	HB	5-10	209	11/11/80	2	North Carolina
43	Troy Polamalu	SS	5-10	212	4/19/81	3	Southern California
46	Arnold Harrison	LB	6-3	236	9/20/82	R	Georgia
50	Larry Foote	LB	6-0	239	6/12/80	4	Michigan
51	James Farrior	LB	6-2	243	1/6/75	9	Virginia
53	Clark Haggans	LB	6-4	243	1/10/77	6	Colorado State
54	Rian Wallace	LB	6-2	243	5/24/82	R	Temple
55	Joey Porter	LB	6-3	250	3/22/77	7	Colorado State
56	Chukky Okobi	C	6-1	318	11/18/78	5	Purdue
57	Clint Kriewaldt	LB	6-1	248	3/17/76	7	Wis.-Stevens Point
60	Greg Warren	LS	6-3	252	10/18/81	R	North Carolina
64	Jeff Hartings	C	6-3	299	9/7/72	10	Penn State
66	Alan Faneca	LG	6-5	307	12/7/76	8	Louisiana State
67	Kimo von Oelhoffen	DE	6-4	299	1/30/71	12	Boise State
68	Chris Kemoeatu	RG	6-3	344	1/4/83	R	Utah
72	Barrett Brooks	RT	6-4	325	5/5/72	10	Kansas State
73	Kendall Simmons	RG	6-3	319	3/11/79	4	Auburn
76	Chris Hoke	NT	6-3	296	4/6/76	5	Brigham Young
77	Marvel Smith	LT	6-5	310	8/6/78	6	Arizona State
78	Max Starks	RT	6-7	337	1/10/82	2	Florida
79	Trai Essex	LT	6-4	324	12/5/82	R	Northwestern
80	Cedrick Wilson	SE	5-10	183	12/17/78	5	Tennessee
81	Sean Morey	FL	5-11	200	2/26/76	4	Brown
82	Antwaan Randle El	SE	5-10	192	8/17/79	4	Indiana
83	Heath Miller	TE	6-5	256	10/22/82	R	Virginia
84	Jerame Tuman	TE	6-4	253	3/24/76	7	Michigan
85	Nate Washington	SE	6-1	185	8/28/83	R	Tiffin
86	Hines Ward	FL	6-0	205	3/8/76	8	Georgia
89	Lee Mays	FL	6-2	193	9/18/78	4	Texas-El Paso
90	Travis Kirschke	DE	6-3	288	9/6/74	9	UCLA
91	Aaron Smith	DE	6-5	298	4/9/76	7	Northern Colorado
92	James Harrison	LB	6-0	242	5/4/78	2	Kent State
96	Shaun Nua	DE	6-5	280	5/22/81	R	Brigham Young
98	Casey Hampton	NT	6-1	325	9/3/77	5	Texas
99	Brett Keisel	DE	6-5	285	9/19/78	4	Brigham Young

Reserve/Injured

No	Name	Pos	Hgt	Wt	Birthday	Exp	College
11	Quincy Morgan	SE	6-1	215	9/23/77	5	Kansas State
33	Russell Stuvaints	SS	6-0	202	8/28/80	3	Youngstown State
94	Andre Frazier	ROLB	6-5	234	6/29/82	R	Cincinnati

Practice Squad

No	Name	Pos	Hgt	Wt	Birthday	Exp	College
18	Walter Young	WR	6-4	220	12/7/79	2	Illinois
42	John Kuhn	RB	6-0	255	9/9/82	R	Shippensburg
45	Richard Seigler	LB	6-2	238	10/19/80	2	Oregon State
47	Ronald Stanley	LB	6-0	244	3/6/83	R	Michigan State
49	Erik Jensen	TE	6-3	236	10/11/80	R	Iowa
65	Tim Brown	G	6-5	313	5/12/80	R	West Virginia
69	Ulish Booker	OT	6-6	309	8/14/79	1	Michigan State
74	Grant Bowman	DT	6-1	300	5/13/80	1	Michigan

STEELERS STATISTICS (FINAL REGULAR SEASON)

PASSING

	ATT	COM	YDS	TD	INT	RATE
Roethlisberger	268	168	2385	17	9	98.6
Maddox	71	34	406	2	4	51.7
Batch	36	23	246	1	1	81.5
Randle El	3	3	67	1	0	158.3
Gardocki	1	0	0	0	0	39.6
TEAM	379	228	3104	21	14	89.4
OPPONENTS	549	315	3480	15	15	74.0

RUSHING

	ATT	YDS	AVG	LONG	TD
Parker	255	1202	4.7	80t	4
Bettis	110	368	3.3	39	9
Haynes	74	274	3.7	20	3
Staley	38	148	3.9	17	1
Randle El	12	73	6.1	43	0
Roethlisberger	31	69	2.2	13	3
Batch	11	30	2.7	15	1
Maddox	8	26	3.3	16	0
Kreider	3	21	7.0	12	0
Ward	3	10	3.3	7	0
Herron	3	2	0.7	1	0
Wilson	1	0	0.0	0	0
TEAM	549	2223	4.0	80t	21
OPPONENTS	402	1376	3.4	36	10

RECEIVING

	NO	YDS	AVG	LONG	TD
Ward	69	975	14.1	85t	11
Miller	39	459	11.8	50	6
Randle El	35	558	15.9	63t	1
Wilson	26	451	17.3	46	0
Parker	18	218	12.1	48	1
Haynes	11	113	10.3	18	0
Morgan	9	150	16.7	31t	2
Kreider	7	43	6.1	9	0
Staley	6	34	5.7	9	0
Bettis	4	40	10.0	16	0
Tuman	3	57	19.0	27	0
Kranchick	1	6	6.0	6	0
Morey	0	0	—	0	0
Washington	0	0	—	0	0
TEAM	228	3104	13.6	85t	21
OPPONENTS	315	3480	11.0	80t	15

INTERCEPTIONS

	NO	YDS	AVG	LONG	TD
Hope	3	60	20.0	55	0
Polamalu	2	42	21.0	36	0
Townsend	2	26	13.0	26	0
Porter	2	9	4.5	9	0
Harrison	1	25	25.0	25	0
Colclough	1	14	14.0	14	0
Carter	1	3	3.0	3	0
McFadden	1	0	0.0	0	0
A. Smith	1	0	0.0	0	0
Taylor	1	0	0.0	0	0
TEAM	15	179	11.9	55	0
OPPONENTS	14	194	13.9	41t	1

STEELERS STATISTICS (FINAL REGULAR SEASON)

SACKS

	NO
Porter	10.5
Haggans	9.0
von Oelhoffen	3.5
Foote	3.0
Harrison	3.0
Keisel	3.0
Polamalu	3.0
Townsend	3.0
J. Farrior	2.0
A. Smith	2.0
Carter	1.0
Colclough	1.0
Frazier	1.0
Kirschke	1.0
McFadden	1.0
TEAM	47.0
OPPONENTS	32.0

PUNTING

	NO	YDS	AVG	IN 20	LONG	BLK
Gardocki	67	2803	41.8	22	65	0
Roethlisberger	2	72	36.0	1	39	0
TEAM	69	2875	41.7	23	65	0
OPPONENTS	80	3463	43.3	19	58	0

PUNT RETURNS

	NO	FC	YDS	AVG	LONG	TD
Randle El	44	12	448	10.2	81t	2
Iwuoma	1	0	3	3.0	3	0
Taylor	1	0	19	19.0	19	0
Harrison	0	1	0	----	----	0
TEAM	46	13	470	10.2	81t	2
OPPONENTS	37	12	336	9.1	36	0

KICKOFF RETURNS

	NO.	YARDS	AVG	LONG	TD
Morgan	23	583	25.3	74	0
Colclough	22	473	21.5	63	0
Taylor	3	59	19.7	24	0
Wilson	3	53	17.7	29	0
Keisel	2	23	11.5	12	0
Harrison	1	-2	-2.0	-2	0
Kreider	1	3	3.0	3	0
Randle El	1	16	16.0	16	0
TEAM	56	1208	21.6	74	0
OPPONENTS	77	1685	21.9	94	0

SCORING

	TDs RUS	TDs REC	TDs RET	XP	FG	PTS
Reed	0	0	0	45	24	117
Ward	0	11	0	0	0	66
Bettis	9	0	0	0	0	54
Miller	0	6	0	0	0	36
Parker	4	1	0	0	0	30
Haynes	3	0	0	0	0	18
Randle El	0	1	2	0	0	18
Roethlisberger	3	0	0	0	0	18
Morgan	0	2	0	0	0	12
Batch	1	0	0	0	0	6
Polamalu	0	0	1	0	0	6
Staley	1	0	0	0	0	6
Foote	0	0	0	0	0	2
TEAM	21	21	3	45	24	389
OPPONENTS	10	15	2	24	24	258

Season Stats

FUMBLES/RECOVERIES

	FUM	OFF REC	DEF REC
Batch	1	2	0
Carter	0	0	1
Colclough	1	0	0
Faneca	0	2	0
J. Farrior	0	0	1
Foote	0	0	1
Harrison	0	1	0
Hartings	1	0	0
Haynes	2	1	0
Hope	0	0	1
Iwuoma	0	0	1
Keisel	0	0	1
Kirschke	0	0	1
Maddox	2	0	0
McFadden	0	0	1
Miller	0	1	0
Morey	0	1	0
Morgan	1	0	0
Parker	4	2	0
Polamalu	0	0	2
Porter	0	0	1
Randle El	4	0	0
Roethlisberger	2	1	0
A. Smith	0	0	1
Staley	1	1	0
Taylor	0	0	2
Townsend	0	0	1
Ward	1	0	0
Warren	1	0	0
Wilson	1	1	0
TEAM	22	13	15
OPPONENTS	30	15	9

SCORE BY QUARTERS

	1	2	3	4	OT	TOT
TEAM	99	121	103	66	0	389
OPPONENTS	78	49	54	68	9	258

FIELD GOALS

	1-19	20-29	30-39	40-49	50+
Reed	0/0	9/9	9/9	6/9	0/2
TEAM	0/0	9/9	9/9	6/9	0/2
OPPONENTS	0/0	8/8	5/8	11/13	0/1